Anomaly Detection as a Service

Challenges, Advances, and Opportunities

Synthesis Lectures on Information Security, Privacy, and Trust

Editors

Elisa Bertino, *Purdue University*

Ravi Sandhu, *University of Texas, San Antonio*

The Synthesis Lectures Series on Information Security, Privacy, and Trust publishes 50- to 100-page publications on topics pertaining to all aspects of the theory and practice of Information Security, Privacy, and Trust. The scope largely follows the purview of premier computer security research journals such as ACM Transactions on Information and System Security, IEEE Transactions on Dependable and Secure Computing and Journal of Cryptology, and premier research conferences, such as ACM CCS, ACM SACMAT, ACM AsiaCCS, ACM CODASPY, IEEE Security and Privacy, IEEE Computer Security Foundations, ACSAC, ESORICS, Crypto, EuroCrypt and AsiaCrypt. In addition to the research topics typically covered in such journals and conferences, the series also solicits lectures on legal, policy, social, business, and economic issues addressed to a technical audience of scientists and engineers. Lectures on significant industry developments by leading practitioners are also solicited.

Anomaly Detection as a Service: Challenges, Advances, and Opportunities

Danfeng (Daphne) Yao, Xiaokui Shu, Long Cheng, and Salvatore J. Stolfo

ISBN: 978-3-031-01226-6 paperback
ISBN: 978-3-031-02354-5 ebook

DOI 10.1007/978-3-031-02354-5

A Publication in the Springer series
SYNTHESIS LECTURES ON INFORMATION SECURITY, PRIVACY, AND TRUST

Lecture #22
Series Editors: Elisa Bertino, *Purdue University*
                Ravi Sandhu, *University of Texas, San Antonio*
Series ISSN
Print 1945-9742   Electronic 1945-9750

Parts of this book are based on the PhD theses of Xiaokui Shu [244], Kui Xu [300], Gabriela F. Cretu-Ciocarlie [65], Hao Zhang [317], Karim O. Elish [77], and the paper [53].

Anomaly Detection as a Service

Challenges, Advances, and Opportunities

Danfeng (Daphne) Yao
Virginia Tech

Xiaokui Shu
IBM Research

Long Cheng
Virginia Tech

Salvatore J. Stolfo
Columbia University

SYNTHESIS LECTURES ON INFORMATION SECURITY, PRIVACY, AND TRUST #22

ABSTRACT

Anomaly detection has been a long-standing security approach with versatile applications, ranging from securing server programs in critical environments, to detecting insider threats in enterprises, to anti-abuse detection for online social networks. Despite the seemingly diverse application domains, anomaly detection solutions share similar technical challenges, such as how to accurately recognize various normal patterns, how to reduce false alarms, how to adapt to concept drifts, and how to minimize performance impact. They also share similar detection approaches and evaluation methods, such as feature extraction, dimension reduction, and experimental evaluation.

The main purpose of this book is to help advance the real-world adoption and deployment anomaly detection technologies, by systematizing the body of existing knowledge on anomaly detection. This book is focused on data-driven anomaly detection for software, systems, and networks against advanced exploits and attacks, but also touches on a number of applications, including fraud detection and insider threats. We explain the key technical components in anomaly detection workflows, give in-depth description of the state-of-the-art data-driven anomaly-based security solutions, and more importantly, point out promising new research directions. This book emphasizes on the need and challenges for deploying service-oriented anomaly detection in practice, where clients can outsource the detection to dedicated security providers and enjoy the protection without tending to the intricate details.

KEYWORDS

anomaly detection, data driven, proactive defense, program and software security, system and network security, outsource, anomaly detection as a service, deployment, data science, classification, machine learning, novelty detection, program analysis, control flow, data flow, semantic gap, inference and reasoning, code-reuse attack, data-oriented attack, advanced persistent threat, zero-day exploit, system tracing, hardware tracing, false negative, false positive, performance, usability, insider threat, fraud detection, cyber intelligence, automation, democratization of technology, Linux, Android, x86, ARM

Contents

Preface

Anomaly detection is one of the few proactive defense approaches. This book is intended to provide an introduction to anomaly-based security defense techniques with a focus on data-science based approaches. The book summarizes the history and the landscape of anomaly detection research, systematizes and contextualizes the existing solutions, explains how various components and techniques are connected and related to each other, and more importantly, points out the exciting and promising new research and development opportunities in data-driven anomaly detection. The book focuses on the anomaly detection in program executions and computer networks. It can be used as a textbook for advanced graduate courses, or undergraduate senior elective courses.

As the need for security is becoming an integral part of the society, we intend to make this book useful and accessible for a large audience, including cybersecurity professionals at all levels, data scientists, usability engineers, and various application-domain experts. Achieving cyber security depends on inter-disciplinary research and development efforts.

The book is titled *Anomaly Detection as a Serice*. It is a grand and ambitious vision that has yet to become reality. Throughout the book, we discuss how current technologies could be extended to achieve anomaly detection as a service and the gaps to be filled. With the unprecedented advances on data science and growing interests from both the academia and industry on anomaly detection, the timing for pushing for this vision could not be any better. We hope this book can encourage and engage researchers, practitioners, and vendors in anomaly-detection related innovations.

The book is organized as follows. The first three chapters introduce the anomaly detection fundamentals. The next four chapters dive into key technical areas, including program analysis, cyber-physical systems, sensemaking, and automation. The last two chapters describe industry development and future opportunities.

A brief summary of each chapter is as follows. In Chapter 1, we give an overview of the field of anomaly detection with a focus on the past, present, and future of program anomaly detection. We also describe the vision of anomaly detection as a service. In Chapter 2, we point out the importance of defining threat models in anomaly detection, and introduce major attack categories against programs, as well as the attacks against detection systems. In Chapter 3, we describe basic techniques for modeling program behaviors, and explain the differences between local anomaly detection and global anomaly detection.

In Chapter 4, we show various ways that insights from code analysis can substantially improve data-driven anomaly detection, including Android malware detection. In Chapter 5, we show how to reason about control-program semantics with respect to the physical environment, which is important for protecting cyber-physical systems. In Chapter 6, we describe several network anomaly detection methods that are all based on making sense of massive amounts of network traffic. In Chapter 7, we show the technical advances in automating n-gram based detection, including automatic calibration, adjustment, and maintenance. In addition, we point out the key requirements for conducting rigorous experimental evaluation of data-driven anomaly detection.

In Chapter 8, we give an overview of anomaly detection technologies in the security industry and point out the anomaly-detection components in various commercial products. In the last Chapter 9, we point out several exciting new research and development opportunities that will help realize the vision of the anomaly detection as a service.

Danfeng (Daphne) Yao, Xiaokui Shu, Long Cheng, and Salvatore J. Stolfo
October 2017

Acknowledgments

I would like to thank Elisa Bertino for giving us this wonderful opportunity to write a book on a topic that I love. We are honored to become authors contributing to Elisa and Ravi Sandhu's series *Synthesis Lectures on Information Security, Privacy, and Trust*.

I would also like to thank my husband Chang, my daughter Radia, and my mother Yuzhu for being so supportive for me while I take on this book project and work on it almost endlessly.

I would like to thank my coauthors for being extremely generous with their time and effort on the book. I also thank Diane Cerra, our executive editor at Morgan & Claypool, for her patience and help. Finally, I would like to thank Office of Naval Research (Grant N00014-17-1-2498), National Science Foundation, and Army Research Office for their funding support.

Danfeng (Daphne) Yao
October 2017

CHAPTER 1

Introduction

1.1 APPLICATIONS OF ANOMALY DETECTION

Virtually all forms of anomaly detection have two implicit assumptions: (i) there is some way to define the normal patterns and (ii) deviations from the norm are indicators of undesirable activities, i.e., anomalies. The concept of anomaly detection is quite intuitive. Therefore, anomaly detection finds its applications in a vast number of distinct settings, for example, insider trading [160, 178, 268], anomaly weather forecast [67, 71], unusual flight paths [243], abnormal quality of service in content delivery networks such as Netflix [37, 138], anti-abuse detection for online activities such as fake accounts and fake YouTube views [29], anomalies in online social networks such as Twitter [151], video surveillance [170], organizational insider threat detection [237], and protection of computer systems, e.g., on file systems [190] and system calls or function calls [249, 302, 304]. Most recently, researchers successfully demonstrated spearphishing detection involving 370 million emails using anomaly detection [125].

Techniques for computing anomalies vary from application to application. The shared challenge is to identify the normal patterns and compute deviations. The most intuitive method is to compute the means and standard deviations, as suggested by Denning [72]. Her 1987 seminal paper was the first to describe the anomaly-based intrusion detection approach [72]. However, this straightforward approach has limited effectiveness in real-world applications, which may have non-numerical data, high dimensional data, time series, or seasonal data (i.e., data whose characteristics change with time). For example, data collected from monitoring programs and systems is usually sequences of events such as system calls, function calls, library calls, or machine instructions that programs make. These sequences may be infinitely long for servers. Online social network data may likely contain structures (e.g., graphs [182]) that need to be incorporated into the analysis. Business transactions and retail activities may be seasonal.

A one-size-fits-all anomaly detection solution is probably impossible. According to a 2009 survey, virtually all existing solutions are tailored for specific types of applications and datasets [46], although some underlying methods may be shared. The question of *What does it take to democratize anomaly detection for domain experts who are not data scientists?* has never been asked before. In Chapter 9, we point out a couple of promising future directions.

In the literature, the term anomaly detection is not defined consistently. Most papers follow the canonical definition of modeling the boundary of normal behaviors and detecting outliers (Type I approach below). However, some works use the term to refer to the detection of pre-specified anomalous patterns (Type II approach below).

- Type I – *Canonical anomaly detection: modeling the boundary of normal behaviors and detecting outliers.* This approach is consistent with the definition of anomaly detection that was first given by Denning [72]. Techniques usually fall into two categories, semisupervised learning (e.g., Hidden Markov Model [222]) where models are trained with labeled normal data, or unsupervised learning (e.g., robust Principle Component Analysis [37]) where the inputs are unlabeled and may contain both normal and abnormal samples. The book is focused on this type (Type I) of anomaly detection approaches.

  Pros: The beauty of these approaches is that the detection is not restricted by the limited number of known anomaly samples, and the model may recognize new anomalies.

  Cons: Although conceptually intuitive, developing anomaly detection that is useful for monitoring large-scale production systems in practice is considerably difficult, for several reasons.

  1. The main difficulty is in identifying *meaningful* anomalies as opposed to false positives (i.e., false alarms, benign events that are misclassified as anomalous).

  2. Anomaly detection on program and system execution requires *tracing*, i.e., intercepting system events (such as system calls, library calls, function calls), which incurs overhead in production systems.

  3. Choosing the optimal algorithms for use in data-driven anomaly detection requires expertise and substantial training and testing effort.

- Type II – *Others: matching specific abnormal patterns or supervised learning-based detection.* For example, researchers found that insider trades may exhibit unique properties, e.g., sell right before stock prices plummet or purchase right before stock prices skyrocket [178], sell strong-performing stocks, or purchase weak-performing stocks [160]. Scanning stock exchange records for these behaviors may reveal potential insider trading transactions [268]. The approach of detecting specific anomalous patterns is similar to signature-based malware detection in anti-virus (AV) scans, where code or behavior signatures are extracted from analyzing known malware. Anomalous patterns may be gathered through empirical analysis.

  Pros: This approach of directly detecting anomaly patterns is relatively straightforward to implement, as it does not require the modeling of normal behaviors.

  Cons: Similar to signature-based anti-virus scans, this approach cannot detect new previously unseen anomalies, e.g., zero-day exploits.

  In supervised learning, a classifier is trained with labeled normal and abnormal data. Supervised learning returns models that maximally separate the class of known abnormal data and normal data.

  Detection based on supervised learning or matching abnormal patterns does not model or enforce normal behaviors. It aims at recognizing known intrusions and anomalies. Thus, the ability to detect zero-day exploit patterns is limited. Strictly speaking, they are not anomaly detection [46].

1.2   COHEN'S IMPOSSIBILITY RESULTS

To appreciate the necessity of outlier-based anomaly detection in solving cyber security problems, one needs to first understand that cyber attacks and defenses are a perpetual cat-and-mouse game. Fred Cohen's seminal work formalized the undecidability results [57]. Intuitively, Cohen proved that it is impossible to determine whether a piece of program is malicious or not. This negative result paints a rather depressing picture for cyber defenders. Compounded by the fact that cyberspace is asymmetric where attackers are hidden, defenders are put in a passive and reactive position. Cohen proved that the following problems are undecidable:

1. the detection of a virus by its code or by its behavior;

2. the detection of the evolution of a known virus;

3. the detection of a triggering mechanism by its code or by its behavior; and

4. the detection of a virus detector by its code or by its behavior.

The proof sketch for the undecidability of detecting a virus is as follows. Suppose that a virus scanner isVirus(P) can determine whether program P is a virus or not. One can then define a new virus program Q whose behaviors always contradict the virus scanner's predictions, as shown in Figure 1.1. Running the virus scanner isVirus input Q reaches a contradiction. Specifically, if the scanner's verdict on Q is benign, then Q will infect the machine. If the scanner thinks Q is malicious, then Q simply does nothing. Either way, Q's actual behavior contradicts the virus scanner's prediction. The other undecidability results can be proved similarly.

```
Program Q
1.    main()
      { ...
2.        if(!isVirus(Q))
          {
3.            infectExecutable();
4.            if (isTriggerPulled())
5.                doDamage();
          }
6.        goto next;
      ... }
```

Figure 1.1: The code of a virus program Q that defeats the virus scanner $isVirus()$ by contradicting to the virus scanner's prediction [57]. In this example, Q does damage only when certain triggering conditions are satisfied.

Cohen's proof strategy is similar to Turing's proof strategy for the halting problem [276]. Intuitively, the halting problem is to determine whether or not a computer program will terminate based on the description of the program and its inputs. An easy-to-follow proof sketch can be found here [120]. Intuitively, suppose that the halting problem can be solved by a predictor Z, then one can create a program X whose halting behaviors always contradict Z's prediction. When Z determines that the program X will halt on certain input, then X will choose to loop forever. Otherwise, if Z determines that the program X will not terminate, then X will simply halt. Thus, X's halting behavior always contradicts Z's prediction.

This 1987 proof of Cohen precisely captures the typical modern day cat-and-mouse-game-like interaction between malware writers and anti-virus scans observed in reality. Before releasing their malware, malware writers would run them against existing anti-virus scanners. If alerts are triggered, they then modify the code and only unleash it until the scanners think it is benign. Despite this negative result, signature-based scanning, with many very well-developed and mature commercial products for various platforms (e.g., Symantec, McAfee, Kaspersky, VirusTotal, Trent Micro, Sophos), still serves as the first line of defense against known malware that may still exist in the cyberspace. However, for some high-value assets that may be subject to advanced persistent threat (APT, described next), this signature-based scanning is clearly not sufficient.

1.3   ZERO-DAY EXPLOITS AND APT

It is costly, in terms of man-hours, to deploy security monitoring measures. Nevertheless, for assets that are of high value (e.g., military or governement facilities, consumer databases) or that have high public exposure (e.g., popular public servers), investing on advanced security protection is a worthy strategy. High-value targets tend to be subject to advanced persistent threat (APT), where the attack goal is usually cyber espionage, as opposed to causing disruptive damages. Attackers may exploit system vulnerabilities, conduct reconnaissance on the target, and covertly steal sensitive information over a long period of time. The exploit may be previously unknown (i.e., a zero-day exploit).

In April 2017, Shadow Brokers, a hacker or a hacker group, leaked a number of exploits in Windows as part of the classified documents obtained from NSA [241]. These exploits, some of which are zero-day, immediately sent waves of panic across the world and prompted Microsoft to release an emergency response stating that most of the vulnerabilities have existing patches and the rest of them (`EnglishmanDentist`, `EsteemAudit`, and `ExplodingCan`) cannot be reproduced on newer Windows operating systems [191]. Some targets were hospitals [27]. Their unpatched legacy systems were hit by ransomeware based on these published exploits.

Another example of high-value systems is the flight ground control and drone control systems. In the Fall of 2011, US Nevada Creech Air Base discovered that their ground control system was infected by a keylogging virus [18]. Luckily, the virus was a piece of common malware, not specifically designed to target the military system. It was discovered by the host-based security system managed by Defense Information Systems Agency (DISA) [75].

In a statement from Air Force officials, the earlier news report stating that it was the cockpits of America's Predator and Reaper drones that got infected [240] was dismissed. The infected ground system is standalone (i.e., air-gapped), separated from the flight control systems that pilots use to fly weaponized drones remotely [18]. Nevertheless, this incident prompted the U.S. military to switch some drone controls' operating systems from Windows to Linux within a few months [168]. In addition, drone units were advised to stop using removable drives, as the source of infection in the 2011 incident was a removable harddrive that stores maps [240].

For these high-value assets, the investment on deploying advanced defenses such as anomaly detection through monitoring executions is well justified. Anomaly detection complements signature-based scanning, and can potentially be more effective against zero-day exploits than signature-based scanning. Besides anomaly detection, the security community has invented a wide range of advanced defenses, including, but not limited to, Address Space Layout Randomization (ASLR) [2], Control-flow Integrity (CFI) [5], Data-flow Integrity (DFI) [42], Moving Target Defense (MTD) [19, 144, 325], software diversity [163], deceptive defense [26, 150, 263], and N-variant [62, 76]. We briefly describe the control-flow integrity and data-flow integrity work next. They will be mentioned throughout the book.

- *Control-Flow Integrity (CFI)* A binary transformation technique was proposed by Abadi et al. to enforce the correctness of control transfers [5]. Through modifying source and destination instructions associated with control-flow transfers, it embeds control-flow policies within the binary to be enforced at runtime.

  Sophisticated modern attacks such as return-oriented programming (ROP) [228, 238] and data-oriented programming (DOP) [130] allow intruders to execute malicious instruction sequences on a victim machine without injecting external code. Some offensive techniques (e.g., [24, 40, 109, 255]) can circumvent existing state-of-the-art detection mechanisms, such as Control-Flow Integrity (CFI) techniques [5] or address space layout randomization (ASLR) [89]. Because of the increasing maturity of CFI technologies (e.g., Intel's Control-flow Enforcement Technology (CET) [44]), the rise of attacks bypassing CFI is likely to occur more frequently in the near future.

- *Data-flow Integrity (DFI)* The data-flow integrity (DFI) property, first proposed by Castro et al. in 2006 [42], refers to the consistency requirement between runtime data flows and statically predicted data flows. The authors demonstrated the detection of both control and non-control-data attacks by DFI enforcement. However, the complete DFI has a high performance overhead (e.g., 103% for interprocedural DFI). Selective DFI protection is more lightweight, but provides incomplete protection [258].

Recent high-profile exploits can enable attackers to accomplish malicious goals without violating control flows or using any sophisticated hacking techniques. One such example is the

Heartbleed attack. Heartbleed leaks sensitive memory content (e.g., private keys) by abusing an unsecure API call. The execution sequences under attack are compatible with expected control flows of the server. Thus, Heartbleed attack does not violate CFI. As it is virtually impossible to guarantee the elimination of all software vulnerabilities before their release, monitoring and analyzing program execution provides important runtime assurance. For example, Shu et al. detected system abuses similar to Heartbleed attacks via frequency and co-occurrence based analysis [250]. Alternatively, fine-grained security checking enforced by static program analysis (e.g., [223]) can also detect memory overread.

Data-driven approaches (e.g., [61, 72, 88, 90, 91, 100, 214, 236, 294, 302, 304]) detect anomalies in program executions based on statistical reasoning, through data mining and machine learning methods. Its advantage in comparison to language-driven approaches (e.g., [84, 85, 106, 107, 289]) is its support for scalable, quantitative, and probabilistic detection. The quantification ability provided by data analysis is unique. It may differentiate numerical properties such as frequencies of events, likelihoods of occurrences, and correlations of events. It may identify program behaviors that are within the permitted boundary of the execution, however, inconsistent with the previous observations. These detection capabilities are necessary for detecting new advanced attacks that do not violate any control flows of programs, e.g., exploits based on data-oriented programming [130], denial of service, and system abuse in general [249].

An *open problem* that virtually all data-driven security techniques face is the lack of formal proofs of security guarantees, partly due to the fact that the models are built on empirical evidences. This issue is likely to be a fundamental limitation of data-driven anomaly detection. A possible direction is to extend formal methods to anomaly detection. A related recent work is the use of model counting, a formal verification technique, for side-channel analysis [28].

1.4   CHALLENGES OF DEMOCRATIZING ANOMALY DETECTION TECHNOLOGIES

Despite the fruitful academic research on program anomaly detection,[1] there is still a lack of systematic understanding and demonstration of real-world deployment. This deficiency is in striking contrast with the maturity of signature-based intrusion detection technologies (e.g., VirusTotal, Symantec AV, Bro, Snort, and many other commercial or open source tools are available). Unfortunately, most program anomaly detection work is limited to small-scale offline trace analysis in lab environments. Several exceptions do exist, e.g., PAYL and Anagram have been deployed by the U.S. government in critical systems [264].

For general-purpose anomaly detection, there appear to be many numerical analysis tools, including robust anomaly detection (RAD) by Netflix [138], the R-based tool by Twitter for analyzing seasonal data [151], and Splunk [139]. However, it is unclear whether they are being actively used on massive scale production data and how key challenges are solved in production

---

[1]An overview paper on program anomaly detection can be found in [251].

environments, e.g., Are these many alerts all meaningful true anomalies? With the abundance of data and computing resources, generating anomalies is relatively easy. However, detecting meaningful anomalies without excessive false alarms is difficult. The role of anomaly detection in the industry is discussed further in Chapter 9.

A continuous task for security researchers is *how to reduce false positives (i.e., false alarms)*. However, a much grander challenge is *how to facilitate the democratization of anomaly detection technologies*. The vision advocated by Yao [308] is to make data-driven anomaly detection as close to off-the-shelf products as possible, with the cloud support. The slow deployment of anomaly detection in production environments is due to multiple factors, which is discussed below.

- **Low usability** Organizations and users who would potentially benefit from *program anomaly detection* technologies do not have readily deployable products (commercial or open sourced) available to them. Key operations, such as system tracing, feature extraction, model training and tuning, and anomaly definition and interpretation, all require deep technical skills and customization, demand manual efforts, and heavily consume computing resources (e.g., training hidden Markov models easily takes days on a desktop computer).

- **Semantic gap** In addition to these technical challenges, seemingly rudimentary tasks, such as defining which specific normal behaviors to enforce and verifying whether alerts are true anomalies, may be daunting. For example, given data streams from thousands of embedded sensors in a smart building, one hopes to detect hazardous events such as break-ins, burglaries, fires, or pipe leaks. Exactly how to analyze the data is not immediately clear. Closing the semantic gap by mapping data anomalies to actual physical events for confirming true positives is non-trivial. Anomalies caused by advanced exploits may be subtle, as attack techniques constantly evolve to evade existing detection, e.g., mimicry attacks [205, 290]. This subtlety also increases the detection difficulty.

- **Lack of standardized evaluation** Datasets and benchmarks are the key for the systematization of the anomaly detection field. Reproducing exploits is technically involved and time consuming, which prevents data scientists from engaging in the field. Existing datasets are limited. We summarize them in Chapter 7.

These challenges also present exciting research, development, and commercialization opportunities, which are discussed in Chapter 9.

1.5   MAJOR DEVELOPMENTS ON PROGRAM ANOMALY DETECTION

1987 Dorothy Denning's seminal paper on anomaly-based intrusion detection [72].

1996 The first series of experimental demonstrations of anomaly detection on system call traces by Stephanie Forrest's group [91].

1998   Data mining techniques were demonstrated for analyzing network intrusions by Lee and Stolfo in [165] and later in [166].

1999   Hidden Markov model (HMM) was used for program behavior modeling to classify system-call segments [294]. This and most follow-up solutions (e.g., using finite state automaton (FSA) by Sekar et al. [235]) belong to local anomaly detection that inspects short call segments (usually 8–15 calls long).

2001   The first program-analysis based control-flow anomaly detection was described by Wagner and Dean [289]. Follow-up work improved on the precision of modeling control-flow behaviors with various static or dynamic program-analysis techniques. For example, in order to achieve context sensitivity, Dyck linked the entry and exit of a target function with its call sites through instrumentation [107], and IAM inlined each callee function's automata into the caller [112]. Feng et al. designed a stack-deterministic pushdown automaton (PDA) to improve both the efficiency and context sensitivity without instrumentation [84].

2002   A mimicry attack against anomaly detection was demonstrated [290]. The attack consisting of a well-crafted sequence of 138 system calls can evade the pH IDS while attacking wuftpd. Another group also reported the similar issue [271].

2005   Control-flow Integrity (CFI) work by Abadi et al. [5]. This paper has inspired a large number of improvements. For example, CFI for commercial off-the-shelf binaries [322], Total-CFI for system-wide enforcement [220], CFI with 2- to 5-fold improvement in the run-time performance [316], and Modular CFI (MCFI) offers to enforce a fine-grained control-flow graph with a low 5% overhead [201, 202].

2005   The demonstration of non-control data attacks was given by Chen et al. [50].

2007   Return-oriented programming (ROP) attack was demonstrated by Shacham [238].

2008   Automatic sanitization of training data was demonstrated [64]. The work was later extended in 2009 to support the self calibration of anomaly detection models [66].

2013   Wressnegger et al. described how to test the fitness of data for n-gram based anomaly detection [299].

2015   Program analysis-guided machine learning models achieved 28-fold accuracy improvement [304].

2015   Global anomaly detection was first demonstrated for server programs [249]. The detection has the potential to defend against data-oriented attacks.

2015 Intel unveiled the new Processor Trace (PT) technology that offered control-flow tracing with a low 5% overhead [142]. In 2016, Intel published its specifications for a new Control-flow Enforcement Technologies (CET) [44], which provided hardware support for preventing control-flow exploits.

2016 Data-oriented programming (DOP) attack was demonstrated by Hu et al. [130]. DOP does not cause any control-flow violations and can bypass CFI. DOP generalizes the non-control-data attacks, and is more flexible than the earlier Control-Flow Bending (CFB) technique [31].

2017 The demonstration of DOP detection in cyber-physical systems (CPS) by Cheng et al. [53].

Figure 1.2 shows some of the major events related to program anomaly detection.

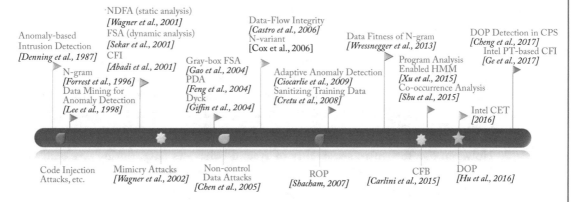

Figure 1.2: Major developments related to program anomaly detection.

1.6   NEW OPPORTUNITIES

In this section, we point out the exciting short-term and long-term challenges in anomaly detection research. We further elaborate on the new opportunities in Chapter 9.

Short-term Challenges:

- *Deep learning for anomaly detection.* Many existing detection solutions (e.g., [249, 302, 304]) are based on memoryless models and are thus order-insensitive beyond the immediate preceding event. For example, they are unable to distinguish cbabc from bcbab, as both of them generate the same set of adjacent pairs {ab, bc, cb, ba}. Deep learning algorithms have the unique ability to recognize complex context (e.g., multiple preceding words) and achieve order-sensitivity. For example, the existing demonstration of natural language translation by Google neural machine translation (GNMT) is remarkable [147]. However, there are multiple technical uncertainties if using deep learning techniques for anomaly detection. For example, it is unclear how scalable deep learning is when analyzing long system traces with hundreds of thousands of calls, which is much longer than sentences in natural languages.

- *Detection of concurrency anomalies.* Many modern services typically have a multi-threaded architecture, e.g., Apache web server.[2] Researchers found 46 exploitable concurrency errors in real-world software, which may result in code injection (e.g., in Microsoft Internet Explorer), bypassing passcode authentication screen in iOS smartphones [307]. Detecting anomalies in concurrent executions has not been demonstrated.

- *Operational issues for anomaly detection deployment.* A collection of tasks that are central to the real-world deployment of anomaly detection technologies need to be addressed. Although seemingly mundane, these tasks may not be straightforward to solve. We give a few examples below.

  1. How can one efficiently update the learned behavior models when the program gets updated? As training is a performance bottleneck, incremental training techniques (e.g., incremental HMM [152]) have been proposed to avoid retraining from scratch. A related problem is automatically recognizing model drift (aka concept drift), which is discussed in Chapter 7.

  2. How can one recognize seasonality of system behaviors (e.g., during weekend and holidays, or before deadlines), in order to build more precise behavioral models and further reduce false positives (e.g., [262])?

  3. How can one replace the slow software tracing with the new fast hardware-level tracing (e.g., using Intel Processor Trace technology [104])? Slow tracing has been the Achilles' heel for program anomaly detection, with multiple-fold slowdown for PIN or strace [308].

Long-term Challenges:

- *Program Anomaly Detection as a Cloud Service.* This anomaly-detection-as-a-service vision was recently pointed out by Yao [308]. Because of the complexity in training and maintaining anomaly detection, the most promising path (if not the only path) to the wide-scale deployment and democratization of the technology is through cloud services. Is it possible for the deployment to be as simple as the just a few button-clicks in anti-virus software? Maybe. What is clear is that the training, testing, and updating processes need to be made automatic and require minimal user interventions.

---

[2]The new Node.js server-side JavaScript environment is single-threaded and is an exception [203].

The key is *intelligence*, making the anomaly-detection cloud smart. Given the client's data (e.g., traces) and security goals (e.g., threat model and accuracy requirement), the cloud providers need to autonomously extract meaningful features, train and test, obtain the optimal detection models, select thresholds to satisfy the client's false positive/false negative preferences, etc. The provider side may rely on the help of security analysts and data scientists, occasionally. However, to be able to serve hundreds of thousands of clients, the anomaly-detection service provider needs to minimize manual effort of the provider.[3]

- *Encyclopedia of anomaly detection.* We coin this phrase to refer to an ambitious direction of exploring all aspects of anomaly detection that are pertinent to its real-world deployment. Its realization will undoubtedly depend on the long-term collective effort and commitment from the research and development communities. Effort toward the encyclopedia may be categorized as follows.

    - *Applications and Threats* (e.g., for healthcare, operational data, infrastructures, computing systems, online social networks),
    - *Algorithms and Parameters* (e.g., SVM, HMM, Decision Trees, Clustering),
    - *Platforms and Environments* (e.g., X86, ARM, Linux, Android, IoT, CPS),
    - *Evaluation and Reproducibility* (e.g., open source and normal, attack, abnormal traces).

SUMMARY

In this chapter, we gave a brief overview of the field of anomaly detection with a focus on the past, present, and future of program anomaly detection. We described the vision of anomaly detection as a cloud service. The effort toward building an encyclopedia of anomaly detection will help systematize the knowledge on anomaly detection and democratize the technology to benefit both organizations and individuals.

---

[3]The current Google cloud machine learning service is not designed to be autonomous.

CHAPTER 2

Threat Models

Defining the threat model is a key step in anomaly detection. It conveys the desired security guarantees of an anomaly detection solution. A threat model describes the adversary's capabilities, e.g., attempting to bypass the password authentication and access a sensitive file. Threat model also clarifies the necessary security assumptions and attacks that are out of the scope. Its dual, security goal, specifies what the defender aims to achieve, e.g., to ensure workflow integrity of a server. In this chapter, we give an overview of security attacks and their manifested anomalies.

Anomalies caused by attacks or security problems are the most useful, e.g., control-flow hijacking, denial of services, bypass authentication, data exfiltration, etc. Unfortunately, anomalies and attacks may not always go hand-in-hand. Reported alerts do not necessarily indicate significant events or attack occurrences. Those alerts, which may be caused by incomplete modeling, are undesirable. Gaining intuitions about the data and threats is an important first step toward high detection accuracy. Attributing the detected anomalies to a specific threat is challenging and usually needs manual effort. Chapter 9 points out the open problem of automating this attribution process.

2.1   FAULTS VS. ATTACKS AND SAFETY VS. SECURITY

Attacks differ from faults in that attacks are purposely caused by adversaries with malicious intentions. In contrast, faults usually refer to hardware failures, operator errors, problems due to design or implementation flaws, or natural disasters. Faults may result in catastrophes (e.g., NASA Challenger space shuttle disaster [45], Therac-25 machine radiation overdose [167]), but the people who are responsible do not have malicious intentions. Fault tolerance research typically concerns safety, as opposed to security. For example, findings in a recent study by Strohmeier et al. about the impact of modern wireless technology on the aviation industry revealed that the *security* of the aviation environment has largely been ignored and oftentimes confused with safety [267].

In this book, we focus on detecting attacks and security (as opposed to faults and safety). Because attacks are intentional, they tend to be more complex, sophisticated, and persistent than faults. Attacks and malware are also evasive in nature and evolves over time to bypass existing defenses, as predicted by Cohen in the 1980s [57]. For example, the evolution of Android malware is well documented, e.g., the code of newer versions of DroidKungFu malware clearly has more obfuscation [324]. Research on fault attacks, which refer to physical attacks that generate hardware faults and can corrupt data confidentiality, belongs to the security category [97].

Faults and attacks may share similar detection techniques. Fault tolerance is an active research field. Its solutions offer important guarantees in real-time systems (e.g., [63, 174, 309]). In cyber physical systems (CPS) and Internet of Things (IoT), both fault detection and attack detection are necessary. However, attack detection usually requires extra mechanisms, e.g., for data authenticity, system integrity, and circumvention prevention.

In the following sections, we describe several categories of threats and attacks, including data-oriented attack, control-flow hijacking, insider threat and data leak, concurrency attack, and mimicry attack. Attacks on cyber-physical systems (CPS) are separately described in Chapter 5 along with CPS anomaly detection techniques. In Section 2.6, we further discuss the impact of the segment length on the attack difficulty of mimicry attacks.

2.2   DATA-ORIENTED ATTACKS

The first data-oriented attack was described by Chen et al. [50]. It takes the advantage of an integer overflow vulnerability found in several implementations of the SSH1 protocol [161]. The vulnerable code is shown in Figure 2.1. An attacker can overwrite the flag integer `authenticated` when the vulnerable procedure `packet_read()` is called. If `authenticated` is overwritten to a nonzero value, line 17 is always `True` and `auth_password()` on line 7 is no longer effective.

Hu et al. demonstrated a much more comprehensive DOP technique that provides data-oriented gadget chaining for completing arbitrary attack goals [130]. Data-oriented programming (DOP) [130] substantially generalizes Chen et al.'s attacks [50]. It systematizes the offensive approach that exploits non-control data. It compromises a program's memory variables, which can be used to achieve a myriad of attack goals, including altering memory permissions, bypassing address space layout randomization (ASLR) defense, and zombifying the victim program (i.e., turning it into a remotely controlled bot). Formally, DOP is Turing Complete, i.e., simulating a Turing machine (namely, assignment, arithmetic, and conditional branch). Attackers can chain together disjoint "gadgets" into an arbitrary sequence. Unlike return-oriented programming (ROP) attacks, DOP does not violate any code pointers, and control-flow execution during DOP conforms to the static control-flow graph (CFG).

Data-oriented anomalies may also be caused by the following attacks.

- Service abuse attacks utilize *legal control flows* to compromise confidentiality (e.g., Heartbleed data leak [122]), and the availability (e.g., Denial of Service attack). Another example is the *directory harvest attack* against a mail server.

- Exploit preparation is a common step preceding the launch of an exploit payload. It usually utilizes *legal control flows* to load essential libraries, arranges memory space (e.g., heap feng shui [259]), seeks addresses of useful code and data fragments (e.g., ASLR probing [239]), and/or triggers particular race conditions.

```
1: void do_authentication(char *user, ...) {
2:   int authenticated = 0;
     ...
3:   while (!authenticated) {
       /* Get a packet from the client */
4:     type = packet_read(); //BOF vulnerability
5:     switch (type) {
         ...
6:       case SSH_CMSG_AUTH_PASSWORD:
           ...
7:         if (auth_password(user, password)) {
8:           memset(password, 0, strlen(password));
9:           xfree(password);
10:          log_msg("...", user);
11:          authenticated = 1;
12:          break;
           }
13:        memset(password, 0, strlen(password));
14:        debug("...", user);
15:        xfree(password);
16:        break;
         ...
       }
17:    if (authenticated) break;
     }
     ...
   }
```

Figure 2.1: `sshd` code vulnerable to the flag variable overwritten attack [50].

- Workflow violations can be used to bypass access control [61], leak critical information, disable a service (e.g., trigger a deadlock), etc. One example is *presentation layer access control bypass* in web applications. If the authentication is only enforced by the presentation layer, an attacker can directly access the business logic layer (below presentation layer) and read/write data.

  Researchers have used state transitions at the application level to detect web server anomalies, e.g., bypassing authentication and payment [61], as well as at the network level for attack discovery in transport layer protocols [145].

Unfortunately, control-flow integrity (CFI) solutions are not designed to detect these data-oriented attacks described in this section. Data-flow integrity (DFI) [42] (in Chapter 1) can potentially defeat these attacks, such as the `sshd` authentication flag overwritten attack in Figure 2.1. However, using DFI to defend against the general DOP attacks has not been demonstrated. The issue is that existing DFI methods are solely based on statically predicted data flows.

It is conceivable that the lack of dynamic data-flow properties such as frequencies may be exploitable for crafting mimicry sequences. In addition, high runtime overhead is another issue that needs to be addressed.

2.3   INSIDER THREATS AND INADVERTENT DATA LEAKS

In 2014, a Navy civilian engineer successfully circumvented U.S. Navy computer security by installing software on his restricted computer system that would enable him to copy documents without causing a security alert. This individual downloaded multiple computer-aided drawings of a U.S. nuclear aircraft carrier USS Gerald R. Ford from the Navy Nuclear Propulsion Information system and attempted to sell them to a foreign government [198]. The specifics about how the authority was initially alerted to this perpetrator's activities are not revealed by the Navy. This type of malicious insider cases, including insider trading [178], existed long before the beginning of digital age [38].

Most of the recent cybersecurity reports [21, 52, 185, 285], including ITRC [143], suggest the trend that insider threats emerge as the leading cause of organizational data leaks, with more than 40% of breaches perpetrated from inside an organization.

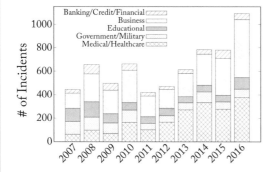 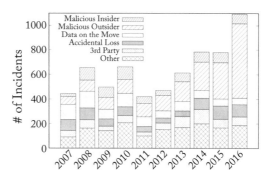

Figure 2.2: Statistics of data leak incidents in recent years (based on ITRC data sources [143]). (a) Breaches by industry sector; (b) breaches by type of occurrence. Figures are from [52].

A large-scale insider-threat analysis was conducted in a real-world corporate database, which involved 5.5 million actions per day from approximately 5,500 users for two months [237]. All collected user data are treated as legitimate activities. The data was collected using a commercial tool called SureView. User workstations are instrumented with SureView. It captures user actions such as logins, file accesses, emails, instant messages, printer usage, browser history, and process usage. Insider threat activities were artificially produced. Table 2.1 gives some examples of the features. However, one of the major findings is that a combination of weak features are more useful for detecting insider threats than a small number of strong features. Unfortunately, the work does not report false positive rates.

Deploying software decoys has been proposed as a countermeasure for the insider's exfiltration of proprietary code [208]. Cloud storage enables the centralized checkpoint for abnormal file and data access patterns, referred to as *fog computing* [263]. International Workshop on Managing Insider Security Threats (MIST) has provided a dedicated forum for researchers since 2009. A book on enterprise insider-threat protection can be found in [59].

Table 2.1: Categories of features with the number of features in each category and an example from [237]

Type	Number	Examples
Email	18	Count of attachments on sent emails
File	28	Count of file events to removable drives
Group	11	Shared printers
Login	4	Count of distinct workstations logged onto
Printer	9	Count of print jobs submitted
URL	13	Count of Blacklist events
Ratio	28	Ratio of file events on removable drives to all file events Ratio of URL uploads to URL downloads Ratio of distinct removable drives to URL up/down loads

Despite the news media's focus on high-profile malicious data breach incidents, inadvertent data leaks due to human errors (e.g., accidental forwarding of sensitive emails, storing unencrypted sensitive data) are surprisingly common. A study from Intel Security [185] shows that internal employees account for 43% of corporate data leakage, with half of the cases being accidental. Content screening and deep packet inspection ensure that unencrypted data storage or network traffic is free of any sensitive information. Research challenges are detection of transformed leaks [252], outsourced detection [246, 248], and parallel screening for scalability [173]. A most recent survey on enterprise data leak threats and detection can be found in [52].

2.4   ATTACKS ON CONTROL FLOWS

The control flow of a program refers to the order of execution, i.e., the order in which the instructions, statements, and calls in the program are executed or evaluated. Control-flow hijacking attacks violate a program's normal order of execution. The well-known code-injection method is shellcode injection via overwriting return addresses, a stack buffer overflow exploit popularized by Levy (aka Aleph One) [9]. The downside of injecting shellcode (i.e., instructions that open a shell preferably with the root privilege) is that the injected code or code segment may be foreign to the native process and be flagged as anomalies.

Code-reuse attacks, including return_to_libc attacks [256] and subsequent return-oriented programming (ROP) [228, 238], avoid injecting new code by repurposing code that already exists in the process image they are attacking. ROP works at the lower instruction level without making function calls, thus is more resilient to defenses or assembler variations than return_to_libc attacks. In return-oriented programming, a gadget refers to a short sequence of instructions that ends with a return instruction. ROP exploits the fact that some architectures (e.g., x86) have variable length instructions with no alignment requirement.

Traditional ROP assumes that the attacker has the knowledge of gadgets locations, whereas attackers in blind ROP (BROP) [24] do not need to have prior knowledge of the vulnerable binary. BROP can remotely find gadgets to perform a `write` system call. The write system call transfers the vulnerable binary over the network to the attacker's machine. Afterward, the attacker can thoroughly examine the vulnerable binary and prepare for further gadget chaining.

ROP attacks have been repetitively demonstrated feasible even with address space layout randomization (ASLR) and other defenses in place [24, 255]. For example, Snow et al. showed a powerful just-in-time return-oriented programming technique, which is an attack based on a just-in-time (JIT) compiler that reads code regions in memory and automatically identifies ROP gadgets on the fly [255]. JIT-ROP bypasses base address randomization, fine-grained ASLR at the instruction, register, and function levels [255], non-executable memory protection, and JIT mitigations. Non-executable memory protection may be denoted by $W \oplus X$ (writable XOR executable).

Multiple demonstrations to bypass control-flow integrity (CFI) also exist, e.g., [40, 109]. These attack-and-defense cycles may not be surprising, given the evolution nature of cybersecurity. What's important is that they confirm the need for inventing and producing proactive defense techniques such as anomaly detection. In Chapter 9, we discuss future work on the detection of concurrency attacks [307].

2.5   MIMICRY ATTACKS

Mimicry attacks [98, 205, 270, 271, 290] differ from the above categories, in that (i) a mimicry attacker has the knowledge of the anomaly detection algorithm and (ii) attempts to evade the detection while accomplishing attack goals.

There are no silver bullets against mimicry attacks that attempt to evade detection by exhibiting near-normal behaviors. One can formalize the reasoning in a proof similar to Fred Cohen's [57] described in Chapter 1.

The first mimicry attack demonstration was given by Wagner and Soto in 2002 [290]. Figure 2.3 shows their crafted mimicry attack sequence that bypasses a 6-gram local anomaly detection tool called pH [257] on `wuftpd` FTP server. The attack exploits a format-string vulnerability, and then calls `setreuid(0,0)`, escapes from any chroot protection, and execs `/bin/sh` using the `execve()` system call. The exploit sequence was manually generated. It takes advantage of the fact that pH (standing for process homeostasis) does not inspect system call arguments.

```
read() write() close() munmap() sigprocmask() wait4() sigprocmask()
sigaction() alarm() time() stat() read() alarm() sigprocmask()
setreuid() fstat() getpid() time() write() time() getpid()
sigaction() socketcall() sigaction() close() flock() getpid()
lseek() read() kill() lseek() flock() sigaction() alarm() time()
stat() write() open() fstat() mmap() read() open() fstat() mmap()
read() close() munmap() brk() fcntl() setregid() open() fcntl()
chroot() chdir() setreuid() lstat() lstat() lstat() lstat() open()
fcntl() fstat() lseek() getdents() fcntl() fstat() lseek()
getdents() close() write() time() open() fstat() mmap() read()
close() munmap() brk() fcntl() setregid() open() fcntl() chroot()
chdir() setreuid() lstat() lstat() lstat() lstat() open() fcntl()
brk() fstat() lseek() getdents() lseek() getdents() time() stat()
write() time() open() getpid() sigaction() socketcall() sigaction()
umask() sigaction() alarm() time() stat() read() alarm() getrlimit()
pipe() fork() fcntl() fstat() mmap() lseek() close() brk() time()
getpid() sigaction() socketcall() sigaction() chdir() sigaction()
sigaction() write() munmap() munmap() munmap() exit()
```

Figure 2.3: A mimicry attack sequence [290].

2.6   SEGMENT LENGTH AND MIMICRY ATTACK DIFFICULTY

Gao et al. performed an exhaustive search to find the shortest mimicry sequence containing a series of six (6) attack system calls (namely, `chroot`, `chdir`, `chroot`, `open`, `write`, `close`) [98]. In the shortest mimicry sequence, these six system calls may not be contiguous. The attack sequence evades n-gram detection (described in Chapter 3). Figure 2.4 shows that the lengths of the shortest mimicry sequences change with the increasing n values. This finding is consistent with the global anomaly detection findings by Shu et al., whose segments are much longer with tens of thousands of calls [249].

In addition, tracing granularity, in terms of blackbox vs. graybox vs. whitebox monitoring, also impacts the mimicry attack difficulty. The more information (e.g., program counter and/or return address) is included in the anomaly detection, the more difficult mimicry attacks become.

Fogla and Lee demonstrated the automatic generation of mimicry attacks to evade network anomaly detection (namely PAYL) [87]. PAYL models the byte- or n-gram-frequency distribution of normal packets [292]. The evasion is called polymorphic blending attack (PBA). An attacker first uses normal packets to probe and learn PAYL's normal profile. Then, the attacker mutates a given attack instance, so that the byte distributions of the final attack packets

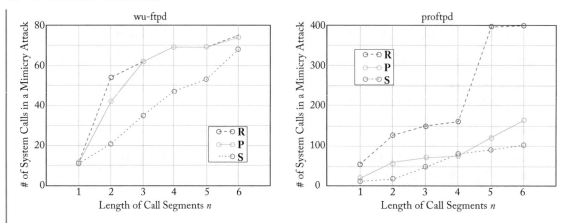

Figure 2.4: Numbers of system calls that a mimicry attack needs to make in Y-axis vs. the length of call segments n in n-gram based anomaly detection in X-axis, for three (3) detection granularities, namely system calls only **S**, system calls with program counters **P**, and system calls with program counters and return addresses **R**. The figures are from Gao et al. [98].

match the normal profile. The mutation operation consists of simple byte substitution scheme and byte padding.

The most interesting result is that Fogla and Lee showed that generating a PBA that optimally matches the normal traffic profile is a hard problem (NP-complete). Their proof reduces the well-known 3-SAT problem to the PBA problem. We further discuss the problem of automatically generating mimicry attack sequences for more complex ML-based anomaly detection in Chapter 9.

SUMMARY

Specifying the threat model is important to anomaly detection. It lays the foundation for building a strong detection solution. In this chapter, we gave an overview of the major categories of attacks against programs, as well as the attacks against the detection systems. When deploying anomaly detection as a service, the threat model needs to be further expanded. Sensitive systems and network traces will be exposed to the anomaly-detection service providers. The privacy risk will be higher, as the provider's machines might be compromised, posing additional threats.

CHAPTER 3

Local vs. Global Program Anomaly Detection

Throughout the book, unless specified otherwise, we will focus on two detection scenarios: (i) one-class labeled semisupervised learning, where the training data is assumed to be free of adversarial contaminations (e.g., [249]); or (ii) unsupervised learning, where the training data may contain detectable noise, e.g., training samples may include old exploits still propagating on the host or the Internet [64]. The latter case usually assumes that the noise is a minority of the training data and they can be identified in the training set and removed from the model (e.g., through detecting outliers or voting) [64, 219, 292]. For example, Cretu et al. demonstrated a micro-model and voting approach to significantly improve the quality of unlabeled training data by making it as attack-free as possible in the absence of absolute ground truth [64]. This technique will be further discussed in Chapter 8.

In this chapter, we explain a key challenge in designing anomaly detection algorithms, namely how to completely incorporate diverse normal behaviors in the model. We highlight some of the existing solutions for both local anomaly detection and global anomaly detection.

3.1 ONE BIG MODEL VS. MULTIPLE SMALL MODELS

3.1.1 MODELING BYTE DISTRIBUTIONS

Wang and Stolfo demonstrated in 2004 the use of byte frequency distribution of network payloads as a model for traffic in PAYL [292]. Their threat model includes worm propagation either at a network system gateway or within an internal network from a rogue device, and more broadly, exploit attempts against services and ports.

PAYL's learning phase produces an extremely fine-grained collection of normal behavior models. It computes a payload model for *each* different length range for *each* port and *each* service and for *each* direction of payload flow. This fine granularity of training produces a far more accurate characterization of the normal payload than would otherwise be possible by computing a single model for all traffic going to the host. In one case, it achieves nearly 100% accuracy with 0.1% false positive rate for port 80 traffic.

The anomaly detector captures incoming payloads and tests the payload for its consistency (or distance) from the centroid model. Encrypted traffic, however, usually exhibits near-uniform distributions, thus PAYL is more effective protecting unencrypted ports and services.

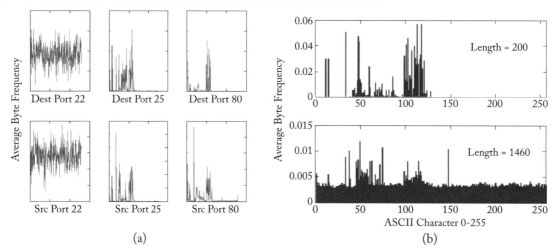

Figure 3.1: Illustration of the importance of having more than one normal model using PAYL [292] as an example. (a) Example byte distributions for different ports, where X-axis is the ASCII byte 0-255 and Y-axis is the average byte frequency. (b) Example byte distribution for different payload lengths for port 80 on the same host server.

Byte frequency distribution of DNS domain names was studied in the context of detecting botnet command and control (C&C) activities [30, 301], specifically on fast flux domains for covert C&C communications. Interestingly, in that context, the authors showed that byte distributions of domain names generated by carefully designed Markov chains are similar to Alexa domains.

3.1.2   MULTIPLE CLUSTERS FOR MULTIPLE BEHAVIORS

Straightforward application of outlier detection methods such as 1-class support vector machine (SVM) rarely works for complex anomaly detection problems, because of the diversity of normal behaviors. In this section, we use LAD [249, 250] to illustrate an example to address this challenge using clustering. LAD, standing for Long-span Anomaly Detection, is a global anomaly detection solution, which will be further described in Section 3.3.

Figure 3.2a shows the very different distributions of function-call traces from seven normal runs invoking `libpcre` with different input strings. `libpcre` is a Perl regular expression matching library. Each distribution is based on the function calls (e.g., `match`) that occur within the `libpcre` library call entrances. Figure 3.2b shows the dismal detection rate of running 1-class SVM alone on libpcre traces. Such a low detection rate indicates that many anomalous traces are misclassified as benign, which is unacceptable.

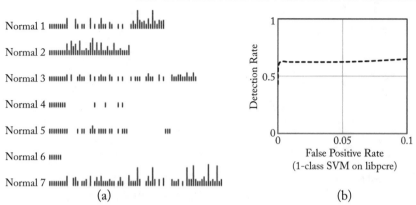

Figure 3.2: (a) Distributions of function-call traces obtained from seven normal libpcre invocations. (b) Detection rate from the straightforward application of 1-class SVM.

One needs to recognize diverse program behaviors with fine granularity, which is particularly important for complex global anomaly detection with long traces, e.g., tens of thousands of calls. LAD utilizes a customized agglomerative clustering algorithm to group similar call traces into a cluster [249, 250]. Then, 1-class SVM based outlier detection is performed within each cluster. Figure 3.3 illustrates how fine-grained behavior modeling improves the detection. Although this two-stage clustering-then-outlier-detection approach is conceptually intuitive (further described in Section 3.3), to demonstrate its feasibility in detecting security-worthy anomalies is technically non-trivial. For example, the agglomerative clustering algorithm needs to balance the sizes of clusters and the number of clusters. Clusters that are too large would not be fine-grained enough to distinguish different program behaviors, whereas clusters that are too small would render the subsequence outlier detection meaningless.

Clustering Options. Support vector clustering (SVC) is a technique that leverages the kernel function in SVM to cluster [20], as opposed to classification. In SVM, a kernel function typically maps a low-dimensional vector into a high-dimensional space, and then uses hyperplanes to partition data in the high-dimensional space to achieve non-linear space partitioning in the original space. This space partition provided by the kernel function in SVM can either be used for clustering or classification.

Although both involving SVM and clustering, SVC and LAD differ fundamentally. (i) LAD clusters behavior instances in the original data space *before* the kernel function transformation. Therefore, the clustering is based on the important semantics knowledge of the data, e.g., call frequencies, co-occurrences, and similarities. (ii) In addition to clustering, LAD performs outlier detection within each cluster using 1-class SVM. This two-stage cluster-then-outlier-detection technique can identify two types of anomalies: inter-cluster and intra-cluster anomalies.

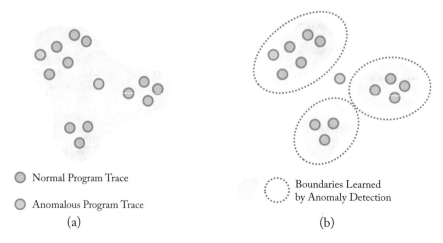

Normal Program Trace

Anomalous Program Trace

(a)

Boundaries Learned
by Anomaly Detection

(b)

Figure 3.3: (a) Straightforward outlier detection may produce a boundary that is too broad and ends up encompassing anomalous data points. (b) Fine-grained clustering differentiates various normal behaviors and improves the detection accuracy, specifically for global anomaly detection.

3.1.3 SUITABILITY TEST

An insightful article by Wressnegger et al. points out three criteria to test the fitness of data for anomaly detection [299]. The purpose of the suitability criteria is to predict whether anomaly detection or classification should be deployed on the data. The criteria include perturbation to characterize the (expected) completeness of training data, density, and variability to characterize the complexity of feature space and data entropy. Intuitively, data with low uncertainty and variations is suitable for straightforward off-the-shelf anomaly detection solutions, such as n-gram or 1-class SVM. The authors' experimental evaluation comparing n-gram-based anomaly detection with binary classification confirms these intuitions.

For example, they found that dynamic JavaScript dataset, consisting of events collected using ADSandbox [74] during the execution of JavaScript code from crawled URLs, has a nearly infinite set of n-grams, and they experimentally confirm that the n-gram-based anomaly detection performs poorly on this dataset, as expected. This work does not consider more advanced anomaly detection techniques, which may improve the detection capability on challenging datasets.

3.2 LOCAL ANOMALY DETECTION

We refer to local anomaly detection as the solutions that inspect short data segments, e.g., 15-call sequences [302, 304]. The threat model for these local anomaly detection techniques is typically control-flow violations.

3.2.1   *n*-GRAM

n-gram is a sequence of *n* items commonly used in natural language processing (NLP) to transform text into features. For information retrieval or text categorization, *n*-grams refer to sequences of *n* consecutive characters or words [70]. Stephanie Forrest's group gave the first demonstration of using *n*-grams in security. They extracted *n*-grams of system calls from program traces and demonstrated such *n*-grams' use for local anomaly detection on system call traces by either simple enumeration [91, 126] or along with their frequencies [294]. *n* values used in their work are small (e.g., 3–15).

Figure 3.4 shows a simple 2-gram example for the enumeration-based detection. The enumeration method is quite strict and leads to false positives if the training dataset is incomplete, as any sequence with new calls or out-of-the-order calls is classified as an anomaly. Although including *n*-gram frequencies in the detection can potentially offer more flexibility and better accuracy, Warrender et al. found the approach, referred to as stide with frequency threshold (or t-stide), performed worse than the enumeration method [294].

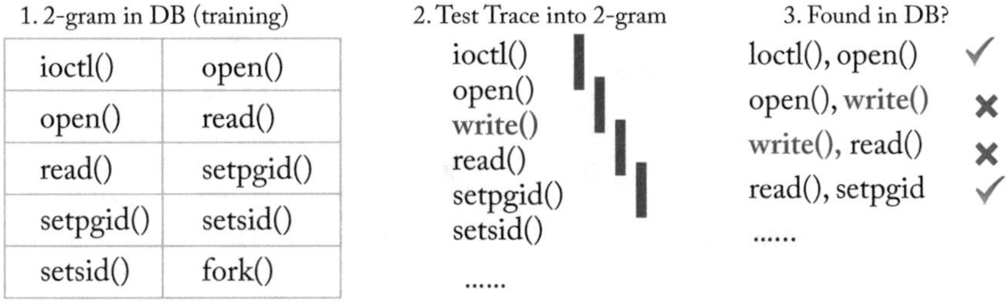

1. 2-gram in DB (training)	
ioctl()	open()
open()	read()
read()	setpgid()
setpgid()	setsid()
setsid()	fork()

2. Test Trace into 2-gram
ioctl()
open()
write()
read()
setpgid()
setsid()
......

3. Found in DB?
loctl(), open()   ✓
open(), write()   ✗
write(), read()   ✗
read(), setpgid   ✓
......

Figure 3.4: A simple 2-gram anomaly detection example.

Anagram, a solution designed for the anomaly detection on network payload, utilizes a Bloom filter for storing and analyzing *n*-grams [291]. During the training, Anagram stores observed *n*-grams in a Bloom filter. During the testing, it computes a risk score of the test sequence based on the fraction of previously unseen *n*-grams (i.e., Bloom filter lookup misses). *n*-gram has also been used on the anomaly detection of library calls [148]. Library calls potentially provide more insights and semantics of the applications than low-level system calls. An efficient open-source version of Anagram called *Salad* is available [298].

Besides anomaly detection, *n*-gram has been widely used as an easy-to-use feature extraction method in other security applications, such as data-leak detection [173, 246, 248, 252], and malware detection in Android [296] or Windows OS [157]. JavaScript malcode detection Cujo [227] and PDF malware detection in PJScan [164] also utilize *n*-grams.

n-gram is designed for local anomaly detection. Supporting extremely large *n* (e.g., 1,000) for global anomaly detection is likely to be problematic, if possible at all. *n*-gram solutions with $n \geq 40$ are likely to have false positives due to incomplete training [251].

3.2.2   HIDDEN MARKOV MODEL (HMM)

A hidden Markov model (HMM) probabilistically represents a memoryless Markov process consisting of unobserved interconnected hidden states, which emit observable symbols [222]. HMM is particularly attractive as an anomaly detection algorithm, as it only needs normal traces from benign executions (i.e., 1-class labeled training data).

Forrest and her colleagues gave the first HMM-based anomaly detection demonstration [294]. They used a (first-order) HMM to recognize legitimate call sequences and compute the likelihoods of occurrences for short system-call segments (*n*-grams). Figure 3.5 illustrates a trained HMM model, where the system calls in traces are observable symbols. The hidden states, denoted by the shapes in Figure 3.5, determine (i) the probabilities of emitting observables and (ii) the next hidden states to transition to. Unlike the observable symbols (i.e., system calls), hidden states do not have concrete semantics and are not observable.

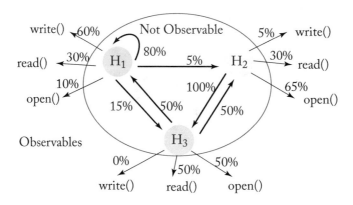

Figure 3.5: An illustration of a hidden Markov model for recognizing normal system-call sequences. The system calls are the observable states. The shapes inside the circle in the center represent the hidden states. The values on the edges represent either transition probabilities among hidden states or emission probabilities between a hidden state and an observable symbol.

There are experimental evidences showing the HMM gives improved anomaly detection performance over *n*-grams [294]. HMM is also more advantageous than the regular automaton model, capable of providing the maximum likelihood associated with a call sequence occurring. Thus, HMM tells not only whether a call sequence is feasible to occur or not, and also how likely it occurs in the normal program execution. Later, researchers proposed using a HMM for comparing two parallel executions for anomaly detection [100]. Authors in [310] systematically investigated the impact of the number of hidden states on classification performance. HMM has also been used for detecting insider threat on CERT insider threat dataset [224].

Although having no concrete semantics, the hidden states can be viewed as representing the internal stages of the programs and their transitions capturing the internal program logics.

Conventional HMM is initialized randomly and solely relies on training to adjust its parameters (namely emission and transition probabilities). Program-analysis based techniques that improve this process are described in Chapter 4. Experimentally comparing HMM with Long Short-Term Memory (LSTM) networks, a deep learning technique, in terms of the ability to recognize the order of sequences is posed as an open question in Chapter 9.

3.2.3   FINITE-STATE AUTOMATON (FSA)

Finite-state automaton (FSA) has been demonstrated to model normal program behaviors for anomaly detection [235]. FSA can capture program structures (i.e., both loops and branches) efficiently and captures an infinite number of sequences of arbitrary length with the finite storage. Researchers found that FSA is particularly suitable for program modeling in cyber-physical systems (CPS) where control programs run in a continuous manner [53].

The construction of an FSA model is based on tracing the system calls and program counters (PC) made by a process under normal execution. Each distinct PC value indicates a different state of the FSA, so that invocation of same system calls from different places can be differentiated. Each system call corresponds to a state transition in the FSA. Since the FSA uses memory address information (i.e., PC values) in modeling program behaviors, it is more resistant to memory corruption attacks than other program models [251].

In an execution trace, given the k_{th} system call S_k and the PC value pc_k from which S_k was made, the invocation of S_k results in a transition from the previous state pc_{k-1} to pc_k, which is labeled with S_{k-1}. Figure 3.6a shows a pictorial example program, where system calls are denoted by $S_0,\ldots,S_6$, and states (i.e., PC values) are represented by integers. Suppose we obtain three execution sequences, $\frac{S_0}{1} \frac{S_1}{3} \frac{S_2}{6} \frac{S_3}{7} \frac{S_2}{6} \frac{S_3}{7} \frac{S_5}{10} \frac{S_6}{11}$, $\frac{S_0}{1} \frac{S_1}{3} \frac{S_4}{9} \frac{S_4}{9} \frac{S_5}{10} \frac{S_6}{11}$, and $\frac{S_0}{1} \frac{S_1}{3} \frac{S_5}{10} \frac{S_6}{11} \frac{S_1}{3} \frac{S_5}{10} \frac{S_6}{11}$, the learned FSA model is shown in Figure 3.6b, where each node represents a state and each arc represents a state transition. In Chapter 5, we use the FSA as an example to explain why anomaly detection models need to be augmented to incorporate physical events and properties for CPS security.

3.3   GLOBAL ANOMALY DETECTION

Global anomaly detection examines much longer or broader system behaviors than the local anomaly detection. The bird's eye view provided by global anomaly detection can reveal stealthy attacks that the local inspection misses. However, the challenge is greater as well. We use a specific global trace analysis solution for server programs, called Long-span Anomaly Detection (LAD) [249, 250], to illustrate the key challenges and how the approach differs from the local anomaly detection.

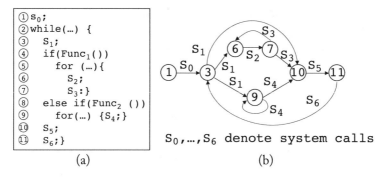

Figure 3.6: System-call-based finite-state automaton (FSA) model: (a) an example program; (b) the corresponding FSA model. Line numbers map to nodes in the program's FSA.

3.3.1   EXAMPLES OF GLOBAL ANOMALIES AND DETECTION ATTEMPTS

Global anomalies that cannot be detected by local anomaly detection or control-flow integrity (CFI) solutions are the most challenging. LAD refers to this category of stealthy attacks as the *aberrant path attacks*. Aberrant path attacks have the following characteristics that enable them to evade conventional detection mechanisms:

- not conflicting with control-flow graphs,

- not incurring anomalous call arguments, and

- not introducing unknown short call sequences.

We categorize four types of aberrant path attacks as follows.

1. *Data-oriented attacks* hijack programs without manipulating their control data (data loaded into program counter, e.g., return addresses). It was first described by Chen et al. [50] (in Figure 2.1 of Chapter 2). The attack was recently generalized by Hu et al. as the *data-oriented programming* (DOP) [129, 130]. DOP utilizes compromised variables to construct loop trampolines and achieve Turing-complete functionalities without directly tampering with control data. In the loop trampoline, a vulnerable variable in a loop branch is exploited to prepare a gadget—a fraction of the malicious payload. The attacker executes the loop trampoline at an unusual pattern to chain a string of gadgets together and achieve attack goals. The attack may exhibit abnormal patterns of the loop usage.

2. *Workflow violations* exploit weak workflow enforcements of a system. The attacker may execute part of the program to bypass access control [61], leak critical information, or disable a service (e.g., trigger a deadlock). One example is bypassing the presentation-layer access control in web applications. If the authentication is only enforced at the presentation

layer, which is not securely coupled to its underlying business logic layer, an attacker can directly access the business logic layer and read/write data.

3. *Exploit preparation* is a common step preceding the launch of an exploit payload. It usually utilizes legal control flows to load essential libraries, arranges memory space (e.g., heap feng shui [259]), seeks addresses of useful code and data fragments (e.g., ASLR probing [239]), and/or triggers particular race conditions.

4. *Service abuses* do not take control of a program. Instead, the attacks utilize *legal* control flows to compromise the availability (e.g., Denial of Service attack), confidentiality (e.g., Heartbleed data leak [122]), and financial interest (e.g., click fraud) of target services.

Before we describe the technique in LAD, let's consider a few alternative approaches and explain why they are inadequate. There are several straightforward solutions providing co-occurrence and occurrence frequency analysis. We point out their limitations.

- **Attempt I:** One may attempt to utilize a large n in an n-gram approach (either deterministic approaches, e.g., [91], or probabilistic approaches, e.g., hidden Markov model [99, 294]). This approach detects aberrant path attacks because long n-grams are large execution windows. However, it results in exponential training complexity and storage complexity. Unless the detection system is trained with a huge amount of normal traces that is exponential to n, a large portion of normal traces may be detected as anomalous. The exponential complexity explains why no n-gram approach employs $n > 40$ in practice [90].

- **Attempt II:** One may attempt to patch existing solutions with frequency analysis components to detect some aberrant path attacks, e.g., DoS. The possibility has been explored by Hubballi et al. on n-grams [132] and Frossi et al. on automata state transitions [96]. Their solutions successfully detect DoS attacks through unusually high frequencies of particular n-grams and individual automata state transitions. However, their solutions do not perform correlation analysis and cannot detect general aberrant path attacks in long traces.

- **Attempt III:** One may attempt to perform episodes mining within large-scale execution windows. It extends existing *frequent episode mining* [149, 165] by extracting episodes (featured subsequences) at all frequencies, so that infrequent-but-normal behaviors can be characterized. In order to analyze all episodes (the power set of events in a large execution window), this approach faces a similar exponential complexity of training convergence as the Attempt I.

LAD demonstrates that modeling the co-occurrence and frequency patterns of a long program trace are useful for detecting the attacks described in this section.

1. *Event occurrence frequency analysis* examines the event occurrence frequencies and the relations among them. For instance, s_1, s_2, and s_3 always occur at the same frequency in Figure 3.7a.

2. *Event co-occurrence analysis* examines the patterns of co-occurred events in a large-scale execution window. Co-occurrence in LAD refers to events taking place within the same execution window, not referring to concurrency. We illustrate an event co-occurrence analysis in Figure 3.7b. $\langle s_1, s_3 \rangle$ or $\langle s_2, s_4 \rangle$ always occur together, but not $\langle s_1, s_4 \rangle$ or $\langle s_2, s_3 \rangle$.

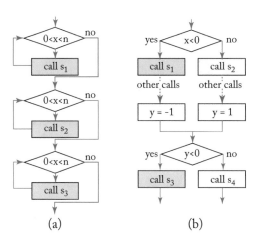

Figure 3.7: Examples of control flows that illustrate co-occurrence patterns and occurrence frequency relations. (a) s_1, s_2, and s_3 occur with the same frequency in a run. (b) The executions of s_1 and s_3 occur in the same run, similarly for s_2 and s_4.

The next few sections highlight the LAD's solution that addresses the key technical challenges in global anomaly detection.

3.3.2   SEGMENTATION AND REPRESENTING INFINITE TRACES

For long-running servers, one needs to break down infinite traces to finite segments before any analysis. Similar to servers, control programs in cyber-physical systems (CPS) run continuously. Thus, CPS anomaly detection also requires segmentation, which is discussed in Section 5.4.2. In LAD, the segmentation is based on the semantics of program behaviors. The authors define an *execution window* as follows.

Definition 3.1   An execution window W is the entire or an autonomous portion of a transactional or continuous program execution.

Execution windows can be partitioned based on boundaries of program functionalities, e.g., login, session handling, etc. Since aberrant path attacks can lead to delayed attack consequences, e.g., non-control data attacks, the analysis needs to be performed on large-scale execution windows. One such window may contain tens of thousands of system calls. An execution window can be obtained as follows:

1. partitioning by routines/procedures/functions,

2. partitioning by threads or forked processes,

3. partitioning by activity intervals, e.g., sleep(), and

4. an entire execution of a small program.

In LAD, a behavior instance b refers to the overall activity of a program within an execution window. A behavior instance is usually very long, which may contain tens of thousands of function/system call events. There may be multiple behavior instances (from multiple runs on different inputs) corresponding to an execution window. Examples of behavior instances used in LAD are as follows.

- Behavior instances in [sshd]: all function calls within routine do_authentication() of sshd (SLOC = 19,215). The routine do_authentication() is called in a forked thread after a client initializes its connection to sshd. All session activities occur within the long trace segment.

- Behavior instances in [libpcre]: all function calls inside libpcre when a library call is made and control flows go into libpcre (SLOC = 68,017). Library calls are triggered through grep -P.

LAD uses two finite-size matrices to represent call traces in a behavior instance, namely a co-occurrence matrix and a transition frequency matrix [249, 250]. The advantage of this matrix representation is compactness. The drawback is that the order information is lost, i.e., the detection does not enforce the order of events within a program behavior instance. The property could be exploited by an attacker. Chapter 9 further discusses this open problem.

Definition 3.2 A co-occurrence matrix O is an $m \times n$ Boolean matrix recording co-occurred calls in a behavior instance b. $o_{i,j} =$ True indicates the occurrence of the call from the i-th row symbol (a routine) to the j-th column symbol (a routine). Otherwise, $o_{i,j} =$ False.

Definition 3.3 A transition frequency matrix F is an $m \times n$ nonnegative matrix containing occurrence frequencies of all calls in a behavior instance b. $f_{i,j}$ records the occurrence frequency of the call from the i-th row symbol (a routine) to the j-th column symbol (a routine). $f_{i,j} = 0$ if the corresponding call does not occur in O.

$$O_{m,n} = \begin{bmatrix} o_{1,1} & o_{1,2} & \cdots & o_{1,n} \\ o_{2,1} & o_{2,2} & \cdots & o_{2,n} \\ \vdots & \vdots & \ddots & \vdots \\ o_{m,1} & o_{m,2} & \cdots & o_{m,n} \end{bmatrix} \qquad F_{m,n} = \begin{bmatrix} f_{1,1} & f_{1,2} & \cdots & f_{1,n} \\ f_{2,1} & f_{2,2} & \cdots & f_{2,n} \\ \vdots & \vdots & \ddots & \vdots \\ f_{m,1} & f_{m,2} & \cdots & f_{m,n} \end{bmatrix}$$

For a behavior instance b, its co-occurrence matrix O is a Boolean interpretation of its transition frequency matrix F, specifically

$$o_{i,j} = \begin{cases} \texttt{True} & \text{if } f_{i,j} > 0 \\ \texttt{False} & \text{if } f_{i,j} = 0 \end{cases} \tag{3.1}$$

Matrices O and F are succinct representations of the *dynamic call graph* of a running program. m and n are total numbers of possible callers and callees in the program, respectively. Row/column symbols in O and F are determined through static analysis. m may not be equal to n, in particular when calls inside libraries are not counted. Bitwise operations, such as AND, OR, and XOR apply to co-occurrence matrices. For example, O' AND O'' computes a new O that $o_{i,j} = o'_{i,j}$ AND $o''_{i,j}$.

3.3.3   INTER-CLUSTER AND INTRA-CLUSTER ANOMALIES

LAD consists of two complementary stages of modeling and detection for event co-occurrence analysis and event occurrence frequency analysis, respectively [250]. Figure 3.8 illustrates the architecture of LAD. Stage I models the binary representation of event co-occurrences in a long program trace represented in the event co-occurrence matrix O for the *event co-occurrence analysis*. It consists of a training operation BEHAVIOR CLUSTERING and a detection operation CO-OCCURRENCE ANALYSIS. Stage II models the quantitative frequency relation among events in a long trace represented in the transition frequency matrix F for the *event occurrence frequency analysis*. It consists of a training operation INTRA-CLUSTER MODELING and a detection operation OCCURRENCE FREQUENCY ANALYSIS.

1. BEHAVIOR PROFILING first breaks down long traces into a collection of behavior instances, and then transforms each behavior instance into a co-occurrence matrix O and a frequency matrix F. Symbols in F and O are retrieved via static program analysis or system call table lookup.

2. BEHAVIOR CLUSTERING is a training operation. It takes the co-occurrence matrices of all normal behavior instances $\{b_1, b_2, \dots\}$ and outputs a set of behavior clusters $\mathbb{C} = \{C_1, C_2, \dots\}$ where cluster $C_i = \{b_{i_1}, b_{i_2}, \dots\}$.

3. INTRA-CLUSTER MODELING is another training operation. It is performed in each cluster. It takes the frequency matrices of all normal behavior instances $\{b_{i_1}, b_{i_2}, \dots\}$ for cluster C_i and constructs one deterministic model and one probabilistic model for computing the refined normal boundary in C_i.

4. CO-OCCURRENCE TEST is an inter-cluster detection operation that analyzes the co-occurrence matrix $O_{b'}$ of a new behavior instance b' against clusters in $\mathbb{C}$. The detection is to find out whether or not there exists a cluster that b' fits in, among all the behavior clusters $\mathbb{C} = \{C_1, C_2, \dots\}$. The clusters are obtained through training in Step 2. If b' is

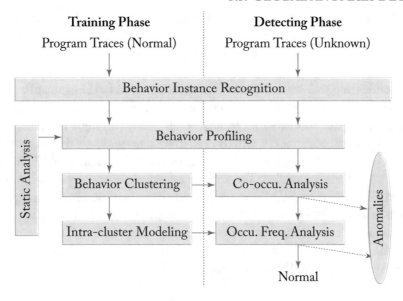

Figure 3.8: Information flows among operations in two stages and two phases of LAD [250].

not compatible with any of the clusters, then it is abnormal. Otherwise, we continue to evaluate b' in the frequency analysis next.

5. FREQUENCY TEST is an intra-cluster detection operation that analyzes the frequency matrix $F_{b'}$ of the new behavior instance b' within a cluster C_i. The cluster C_i is the cluster that b' belongs to in the co-occurrence test above. The behavior instance b' is normal, if and only if its $F_{b'}$ abides by the rules extracted from C_i and $F_{b'}$ is within the normal boundary established in C_i. In LAD, this frequency test is only applied to instances that have passed the co-occurrence test.

This workflow enables LAD to detect multiple types of anomalies and attacks, including the following.

- Inter-cluster anomalies, specifically *montage anomalies*. A montage anomaly is a type of anomalous program behaviors that are composed of multiple legitimate control-flow fragments, but are incompatible in a single execution.

- Intra-cluster outliers, specifically *frequency anomalies*. A frequency anomaly is a type of anomalous program behaviors with abnormal ratios or relations in terms of occurrence frequencies.

LAD achieves promising accuracy results (100% detection rate and 0.01% false positive rate) against reproduced 3 groups of real-world attacks (bypass authentication, directory harvesting, and regular expression DoS) on complex programs (sshd, sendmail, and libpcre), respectively. The authors also compared LAD with a n-gram detection. For example, for the sshd flag variable overwritten attack, a 37-gram model results in a false positive rate of 6.47%. This high FP rate likely indicates that it is difficult for n-gram models with a large n to converge at training.

Besides evaluating real-world attacks, the authors tested LAD against four types of synthetic anomalies. The types of synthetic anomalies include (i) montage anomaly that fuses call paths, (ii) incomplete path anomaly that truncates call paths, (iii) high-frequency anomaly that has high frequency of call occurrences, and (iv) low-frequency anomaly that has low frequency of call occurrences [249]. The traces from of the three programs (sshd, sendmail, and libpcre are used to generate synthetic anomalies. The authors experimentally compared LAD with a basic one-class SVM. The one-class SVM was configured as the one used in the Intra-cluster Modeling operation of LAD. We present the detection accuracy results on libpcre in Figure 3.9. libpcre has the most complicated behavior patterns. In any subfigure of Figure 3.9, each dot is associated with a false positive rate (multi-round 10-fold cross-validation with 10,000 test cases) and a detection rate (1,000 synthetic anomalies). We denote an anomaly result as a pos-

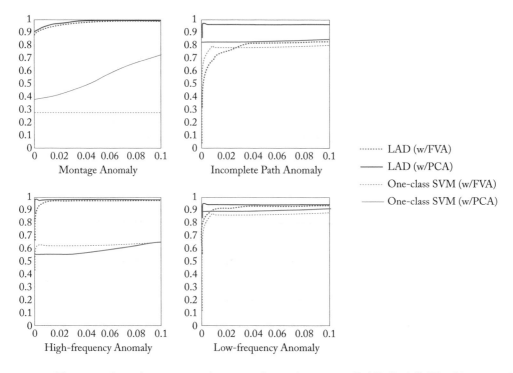

Figure 3.9: The use of synthetic anomaly traces for evaluation in LAD [250]. The libpcre ROC curves of the LAD approach and the basic one-class SVM. The X-axis is false positive rate, and the Y-axis is detection rate.

itive. Figure 3.9 shows the effectiveness of LAD clustering design. The detection rate of LAD with PCA used for feature selection is consistently higher than the other methods. The basic one-class SVM performs poorly for this global anomaly detection task, as expected. Its low detection rates indicate that the one-class SVM model fails to recognize diverse normal behavior patterns.

SUMMARY

In this chapter, we introduced basic techniques for modeling program behaviors. We explained the differences between local anomaly detection and global anomaly detection. They are complementary to each other, equally necessary for security. Global anomaly detection faces bigger complexity and accuracy challenges. As this chapter showed, even the basic anomaly detection solutions require one to have the intimate knowledge about the assets being monitored. Therefore, self calibration, automation, and outsourcing will be the key to the wide deployment of anomaly detection solutions.

CHAPTER 4

Program Analysis in Data-driven Anomaly Detection

Leveraging the insights obtained from program analysis can greatly improve the quality of modeling. In this chapter, we illustrate this point by describing a couple of examples that use static program analysis in machine learning algorithms. The related description on using static dependency analysis for securing control programs in cyber-physical systems (CPS) is given in Chapter 5.

4.1 SECURITY IMPACT OF INCOMPLETE TRAINING DATA

Program behavior models constructed solely through learning from program traces (e.g., [235, 294]) skew toward the limited training data, hurting the detection accuracy. For modern complex software it is extremely challenging to obtain traces with close-to-full branch, statement, or def-use coverage. As shown in Table 4.1, it is typical to have 50–60% coverage for a test-case generation [253, 274]. Incomplete training results in excessive false alarms in a learning-based anomaly detection system, as legitimate call sequences not seen in the training set will not be recognized.

Table 4.1: Program coverage of a well-known testcase suite SIR [253]

Program	# of Test Cases	Branch Coverage	Line Coverage
flex	525	81.3%	76.0%
grep	809	58.7%	63.3%
gzip	214	68.5%	66.9%
sed	370	72.3%	65.6%
bash	1,061	66.3%	59.4%
vim	976	55.0%	51.9%

In contrast to machine-learning based models, program behavioral models developed through static code analyses on control flows (e.g., [112, 289]) are *complete* in that all the statically feasible paths can be predicted. However, because of the lack of run-time information, statically constructed behavioral models cannot distinguish path frequencies. That is, paths with different occurrence frequencies are indistinguishable. This lack of quantification in program behavior modeling, such as [84, 107, 112, 289], can cause important signs of run-time program misuses or undesirable program-behavior changes to be ignored. In addition, binary-instrumentation based control-flow integrity (CFI) techniques [5] are not designed to offer quantitative behavior classification, either.

Next, we present a toy example in Figure 4.1 to further illustrate the pros and cons of these two approaches, and motivate the hybrid solutions (namely STILO [302, 304]) described in the next section.

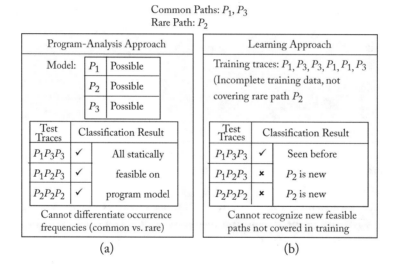

Figure 4.1: Limitations of static program analysis approach in (a) and machine-learning-based approach in (b) [304].

Suppose a function or program has three execution paths (P_1, P_2, P_3), where paths P_1 and P_3 are likely to occur during the program execution. Although statically feasible, P_2 has a very low probability to be executed.

For a learning-based approach, program behavior models are constructed based on system traces that are collected when a clean version of the program executes.

- (*Pro*) It can approximate the likelihood of occurrences for program behavioral patterns. If using a probabilistic representation for call sequences such as a hidden Markov model, it can differentiate frequencies of occurrences, improving detection sensitivity. The model may compute a probability $P(\langle c_1, \ldots, c_k \rangle | \lambda)$ for an observed call sequence $\langle c_1, \ldots, c_k \rangle$ for a given hidden Markov model λ. A larger probability indicates more likely for the call sequence to occur in normal program execution. It can identify feasible-but-unlikely sequences (e.g., $P_2 P_2 P_2$).

- (*Con*) Incomplete training can result in false alarms. As shown in Figure 4.1b, system call sequences containing the rare-but-statically-feasible path P_2 may be misclassified as abnormal.

For a program-analysis based approach, feasible control flow information is extracted through statically analyzing the code.

- (*Pro*) It can discover all statically feasible execution paths.

- (*Con*) It cannot differentiate the likelihoods of occurrences among feasible paths. As shown in Figure 4.1a, a highly unlikely call sequence $P_2 P_2 P_2$ (an indicator of possible exploits) cannot be detected.

4.2   PROGRAM ANALYSIS FOR GUIDING CLASSIFIERS

Most ML-based security solutions do not involve program analysis, or vice versa. Program anomaly detection offers unique opportunities for the two paradigms to intersect. Many machine learning models are initialized randomly, i.e., the initial parameters are chosen randomly or arbitrarily without justification and are adjusted and improved during training. However, poorly chosen initial parameters may mislead the training process and converge at an undesired local optimum.

In this section, we give an example of using program analysis for guiding the machine learning classifiers. Specifically, we present STILO [304] and its context-sensitive version STILO-context [302] that use statically obtained control flows to initialize hidden Markov model (HMM) probabilities. The intuition behind their design is that rather than training blindly from a random starting point, one can utilize the order of execution information extracted from program analysis to provide the guidance to the HMM classifier. The authors set two goals for designing program behavior models for anomaly-based detection.

- To use probabilistic reasoning to ascertain the likelihoods of occurrences.

- To cover both static and dynamic control-flow behaviors.

The authors find a connection between control-flow graphs and hidden Markov model, through quantitative matrix representations. It requires one to approximate and encode control-flow information in a matrix. It involves several definitions as follows.

Definition 4.1   The control-flow graph (CFG) of a function is a directed graph, where nodes represent code blocks of consecutive instructions identified by static program analysis, and directed edges between the nodes represent execution control flow, such as conditional branches, and calls and returns [304]. Calls include system calls, library calls or user-defined function calls.

Consider an edge $(n_1 \rightarrow n_2)$ in a control-flow graph, we refer to n_1 as the parent node and n_2 the child node. A CFG node may or may not make a call. E.g., in the simple control-flow graph of function $f()$ shown in Figure 4.2, node 3 calls syscall `write`; node 5 does not make any syscalls. ϵ and ϵ' represent the external call site and return site of function $f()$.

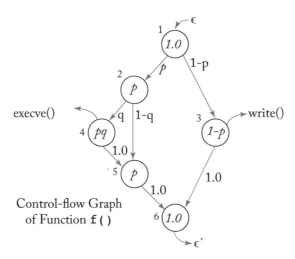

Figure 4.2: Examples of conditional probabilities and reachability probabilities for function $f()$ [304]. Conditional probability of a node pair is shown on the edge. Reachability probability of a node is shown in the node. ϵ and ϵ' represent the external call site and return site of $f()$.

4.2.1 QUANTIFYING CONTROL-FLOW GRAPH

In order to quantify control-flow graphs, STILO defines several types of probabilities. The purpose of defining these probabilities is two-fold: (i) to quantify a program's statically inferred control-flow properties, and (ii) to be compatible with HMM parameters. The values include the conditional probability of adjacent CFG nodes, the reachability probability from the function entry, and most importantly transition probability for a call pair.

Definition 4.2   The conditional probability P_{ij}^c of adjacent CFG nodes for a node pair (n_i, n_j) or $(n_i \rightarrow n_j)$ is the probability of occurrence for node n_j, conditioning on that its immediate preceding node n_i has just been executed, i.e., $P[n_j|n_i]$ [304].

Definition 4.3   The reachability probability P_i^r for a CFG node n_i is the likelihood of the function's control flow reaches node n_i, i.e., the likelihood of n_i being executed within this function [304].

We illustrate the probability values for a simple control-flow graph for a function $f()$ in Figure 4.2. Let p be the probability that the left leg is taken at the first branch, and q be the probability that the left leg is taken at the second branch. Then, the reachability probability P_5^r for node 5 is computed as $pq * 1 + p * (1 - q) = p$, where pq and p are the reachability probabilities of its two parents, and 1 and $1 - q$ are the conditional probabilities with respect to the two incoming control-flow edges of node 5. The algorithm for computing the probabilities can be found in [304].

Call-transition matrix (in Definition 4.5) is the key enabler in STILO to interface with HMM. The definition is based on the transition probability, which is described in Definition 4.4. Table 4.2 shows the call-transition matrix of the function in Figure 4.2.

Table 4.2: A call-transition matrix [304] of the function $f()$ in Figure 4.2. p and q are branch probabilities as shown in Figure 4.2. ϵ represents the external caller of this function. ϵ' represents the external return site.

	ϵ'	write	execve
ϵ	p(1-q)	1-p	pq
write	1-p	0	0
execve	pq	0	0

Definition 4.4   The transition probability P_{ij}^t of call pair (c_i, c_j) in function $f()$ is defined as the likelihood of occurrence of the call pair during the execution of the function.

Definition 4.5   Call-transition matrix of a function stores pair-wise call-transition probabilities of the function. The rows and columns of the matrix correspond to calls that appear in the control-flow graph of the function, respectively. A cell (c_i, c_j) stores the likelihood of occurrence for call pair $(c_i \rightarrow c_j)$, i.e., transition probability P_{ij}^t.

Statically approximating these probabilities of programs following these above definitions allows one to interface with the hidden Markov model. STILO computes the likelihoods of occurrence for call pairs in a function, i.e., transition probability, based on reachability probabilities. In addition, STILO aggregates multiple call-transition matrices, each corresponding to a function, into one much larger complete call-transition matrix representing the entire program. Aggregation operation takes as inputs (i) the call graph of the program and (ii) call-transition matrix for each function. The call graph is needed for the calling relations among functions. We refer readers to [304] for the details of the aggregation operation. The next section further explains how STILO bridges program analysis with machine learning techniques.

4.2.2   INTERFACING WITH MARKOV MODEL

STILO is initialized with call-transition information extracted from static control-flow analysis. This new initialization approach is in clear contrast to the conventional one, as regular HMMs arbitrarily choose the hidden states and randomly initialize the probabilities. The knowledge extracted from program analysis enables HMM to start at a better starting point and converge at an improved optimum. When evaluating against Linux server and utility programs, STILO reports up to 28-fold of improvement in detection accuracy over the state-of-the-art HMM-based anomaly detection [304].

Hidden States. STILO's novelty is giving semantic meanings to HMM's hidden states. Hidden states represent the logical reasons or program phases governing the actions of a program. For example, if one associates a hidden state with a distinct system call or library call in the call-transition matrix (in Definition 4.5), then there is a one-to-one correlation between hidden states and calls in the program. This correlation allows one to configure HMM in a way that more precisely reflects the program's behaviors. In STILO, the number N of hidden states is the total number of distinct calls in the program code. This design choice enables us to conveniently incorporate statically obtained information into HMM. In regular HMM-based anomaly detection (e.g., [294, 310]), N is the number of distinct calls in program traces (which is usually smaller).[1]

Observable symbols. For observable symbols, STILO defines the observable symbols M as system calls or library calls. Thus, they are directly associated with observable program behaviors.

Various Probabilities. STILO's state-transition probabilities $\{A\}$ are initialized with the transition probabilities $\{P_{ij}^t\}$ of call pairs in the program's aggregated call-transition matrix. STILO also has a specialized mechanism for assigning the initial emission probabilities, which represent the likelihoods of emitting observable symbols by hidden states. For each hidden state i, STILO assigns a high emission probability (e.g., 0.5) for the call that i corresponds to, and assigns random low probabilities to the rest of the observable symbols. Because of the one-to-one correlation between hidden states and calls, the initial distribution π of hidden states can be assigned based on the program's call-transition matrix.

Besides anomaly detection, researchers have also proposed probabilistic techniques for programming and software problems, such as vulnerability analysis for software testing [260] and fault localization for debugging [15, 16].

---

[1]Experiments show a larger N does not guarantee the improvement in classification.

4.2.3   IMPROVING CONTEXT SENSITIVITY

The above STILO model is context-insensitive. Context-insensitive program anomaly detection models only record names of calls, e.g., `<call_name>`. Such context-insensitive models rely on flow sensitivity to capture the order and frequency of normal call sequences, and detect anomalies by identifying and classifying call sequence patterns.

An improvement, dubbed the STILO-context model [302], is to record the caller function of each library or system call as the context environment. An observed call invocation can be represented as `call_name@caller_function`. Figure 4.3 gives such a 1-level calling context-sensitive control-flow graph. We demonstrate the effectiveness and feasibility of such context information in probabilistic program anomaly detection.

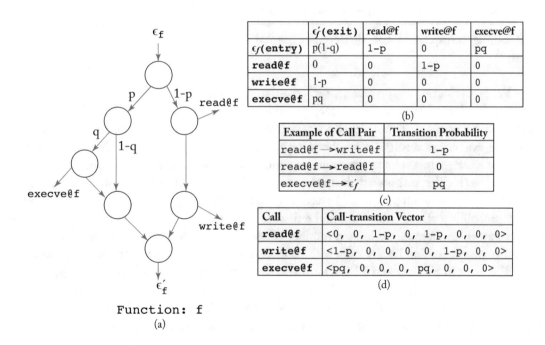

	ϵ_f'(exit)	read@f	write@f	execve@f
ϵ_f(entry)	p(1-q)	1-p	0	pq
read@f	0	0	1-p	0
write@f	1-p	0	0	0
execve@f	pq	0	0	0

(b)

Example of Call Pair	Transition Probability
read@f →write@f	1-p
read@f →read@f	0
execve@f→ ϵ_f'	pq

(c)

Call	Call-transition Vector
read@f	<0, 0, 1-p, 0, 1-p, 0, 0, 0>
write@f	<1-p, 0, 0, 0, 0, 1-p, 0, 0>
execve@f	<pq, 0, 0, 0, pq, 0, 0, 0>

(d)

Function: f
(a)

Figure 4.3: For STILO-context, examples of control-flow graph for function $f()$ in (a), call-transition matrix in (b), transition probabilities in (c), and call-transition vectors in (d) [302]. The call-transition vector of a call is the concatenation of the row and column of that call.

In the following example, S_1 gives a normal call sequence with the right context information, which is their caller function **g** and **f**. Suppose the corresponding program has a vulnerability and fails to check the boundary before the **read** call in function **f**, which would lead to a buffer overflow. An exploitation using this security flaw can launch a code-reuse mimicry attack that makes the same call sequence to fool a context-insensitive detection.

For a detection model that is flow-sensitive, but context-insensitive, both normal call sequence and abnormal call sequence are observed the same as `read`→ `read`→ `write`→ `execve`, thus the anomaly cannot be detected. Code-reuse attack makes use of the existing code inside the entire process memory. Thus, it is highly likely that an attacker uses calls that are from different places within different caller functions. In a context-sensitive model, the incorrect caller information as in S_2 can be easily identified.

S_1: normal call sequence:
... $\rightarrow$ read@g $\rightarrow$ read@f $\rightarrow$ write@f $\rightarrow$ execve@g $\rightarrow$ ...

S_2: abnormal call sequence (code-reuse attack):
... $\rightarrow$ read@g $\rightarrow$ read@f $\rightarrow$ write@foo $\rightarrow$ execve@bar $\rightarrow$ ...

With calling context, one can distinguish normal call sequence (top) from attack sequence (bottom).

When evaluating against Linux server and utility programs, STILO-context shows close to three (3) orders of magnitude accuracy improvement for library calls, and 10-time improvement for system calls on average over context-insensitive counterparts. Figure 7.6 in Chapter 7 shows the evaluation results on synthetic traces. In addition, the authors also show the low number of ROP gadgets in a program under context-sensitive detection, far from being Turing complete [302]. The authors attribute the improved accuracy of the models to the effectiveness of the program-analysis-guided behavior modeling, including: (i) an informed set of initial HMM probability values (transition and emission probabilities and probability distribution of hidden states), and a more optimized number of hidden states; and (ii) a stronger enforcement on legitimate system and library calls with context sensitivity in the program behavior model.

The work in STILO and STILO-context integrates the two paradigms of program analysis and machine learning for anomaly detection. Program analysis significantly enhances the detection capabilities of learning-based methods. The work presents a new approach for constructing program behavior models to defend against stealthy exploits.

4.3   PROGRAM ANALYSIS FOR ANDROID MALWARE DETECTION

Anomaly detection solutions for Android malware detection are relatively new. Most approaches belong to binary classification that requires two-class labeled training data (e.g., [14, 49, 296, 297]). However, there are a few exceptions [78, 321].

In this section, we describe a highly accurate classification approach for detecting malicious Android apps. The method uses static program analysis to extract apps' data-flow features for classification [78]. The features represent how user inputs trigger the invocations of Android sensitive APIs in normal apps. DR-Droid adopts this feature in its detection for repackaged Android malware, where malware writers statically inject malicious code to (popular) benign apps and advertise the repackaged apps as new ones on the market [275].

4.3.1   ANDROID THREAT MODEL AND NATIONAL SECURITY

Besides numerous civilian uses, mobile apps are a critical enabler for the military and government of a nation. They give new opportunities to improve mission effectiveness. However, the dissemination of mobile apps for critical missions demands multiple types of restrictions. First, mobile app stores are private and have restricted access. Only authorized users can download the apps. More importantly, apps need to undergo an in-depth vetting and analysis process before they are made available at the private app stores. Examples of such private app stores include U.S. Department of Defense's Mobile Application Store (MAS) [184] and CIA's private app store hosted by Amazon Web Services [56].

Malicious Android apps may seriously threaten *data confidentiality*, *data integrity*, and *system abuse*.   Compromised data confidentiality may lead to the leak of sensitive information (such as location, unique device ID) on the mobile device. Compromised data integrity is where spoofed information is fed to the user, e.g., fake GPS signals or maps misleading a military convoy [315] possibly via intent spoofing [54, 172]. System abuse by malicious apps (e.g., sending spam, launching DoS attacks, aggressive battery use) does not necessarily compromise sensitive data; nevertheless, abusing system resources is undesirable [78].

The danger of Android malware is that the malicious code may be deeply disguised, i.e., trojanized. They appear to provide useful functionality; however, they may conduct stealthy malicious activities such as botnet command-and-control, data exfiltration, or DDoS attacks. The user-trigger dependence (UTD) work [78] described next is one of the first program-analysis based solutions for screening and vetting Android apps.

4.3.2   DATA-DEPENDENCE GRAPH AND ANDROID MALWARE EXAMPLES

In mobile apps, sensitive operations (e.g., turn on the camera or microphone) typically require the explicit initiation by users' specific actions (or *triggers*). In other words, normal app behaviors are likely to exhibit this dependence relations—operations triggered by user actions. User-trigger dependence (UTD) based security leverages this dependence relations between user inputs/actions and sensitive API calls providing critical system functions for static anomaly detection in Android apps [78].

Next, we explain several program analysis concepts used in UTD and use examples to illustrate the detection mechanism. A data dependence graph (DDG) represents a program's inter-procedural data flows [128]. DDG differs from a control-flow graph, which describes the order of program execution. The DDG is a directed graph representing data dependence between program instructions, where a node represents a program instruction (e.g., assignment statement), and an edge represents the data dependence between two nodes. The data dependence edges are identified by data-flow analysis. A direct edge from node n_1 to node n_2, which is denoted by $n_1 \rightarrow n_2$, means that n_2 uses the value of variable x which is defined by n_1. Formally, let I be the set of instructions in a program P. The data dependence graph G for program P is denoted by $G = [I, E]$, where E represents the directed edges in G, and a directed edge $I_i \rightarrow I_j \in E$ if there is a def-use path from instructions I_i to I_j with respect to a variable x in P. Def-use is short for definition and use in data-flow analysis.

For example, Figure 4.4a shows a partial def-use dependence graph for a real-world Android malware HippoSMS, which affects Android smartphones by subscribing to premium SMS services. The malware sends SMS messages to a hard-coded premium-rated number without the user's knowledge. sendTextMessage() is a sensitive API call. Figure 4.4a shows that sendSMS(p0, p1, p2) method is called with a hard-coded premium-rated number 1066156686 as its p0 argument. The subsequent sendSMS method calls a sensitive API sendTextMessage() with the same hard-coded value p0 as its phoneNum argument. However, there is no direct dependence path between the sendTextMessage() API call and any user inputs (e.g., data and actions), which indicates abnormal.

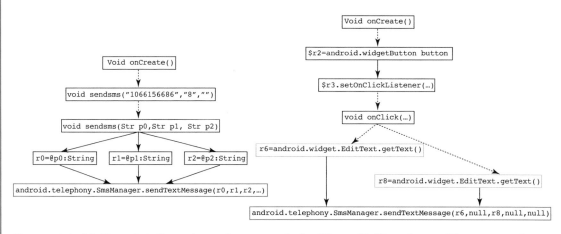

Figure 4.4: (a) Partial def-use dependence graph for HippoSMS malware. There is no direct path showing a dependency between user triggers and sendTextMessage(). (b) Partial def-use dependence graph for a legitimate app. sendTextMessage() has the required user dependence property. User triggers are shown in green nodes. Figures are from [78].

Another example in Figure 4.4b shows the partial def-use dependence graph of a legitimate app for sending SMS messages [78]. The graph indicates that the API call sendTextMessage() depends on the some inputs from the user, as one of its argument is entered by the user via text fields, through getText() API. There are direct dependence paths between user inputs (e.g., data and actions) and the sendTextMessage() API.

Android provides a large number of user interface components. Each of them has its corresponding triggering function. A `Button` object is concatenated with the `onClick` function, and a `Menu` object can be concatenated with the `onMenu-ItemClick` function. Malicious apps may invoke critical APIs without user interactions. User interaction features represent the interaction frequency between the app and users.

4.3.3   USER-TRIGGER DEPENDENCE-BASED DETECTION

In the Java bytecode of an Android app, UTD labels sensitive user-action related APIs as *sources*, and labels critical operation related APIs as *sinks* [78]. It performs inter-procedural data-flow analysis to extract dependence properties between the sensitive sources and sinks, and quantifies them for classification. Existing program analysis solutions cannot be directly applied to solve the problem, in part because of the lack of proper handling of Android-specific features such as Intents.

We first give the definitions for the terminology used in the classification, including *operation*, *trigger*, *dependence path*, and *valid call site* [78].

An operation is an API call which refers to a function call providing system service such as network I/O, file I/O, telephony services in the program [78]. The work focuses on a subset of function calls—the critical API calls that can be used for accessing private data and utilizing system resources. Examples of the operations are send/receive network traffic, create/read/write/delete operations for files, insert/update/delete operations in database and content provider, execute system commands using `java.lang.Runtime.exec`, access and return private information such as location information and phone identifiers, and send text messages in telephony services.

A trigger refers to a user's input or action/event on the app [78]. A trigger is a variable defined in the program. For example, the user's input may be text entered via a text field, while the user's action/event is any click on UI element, such as a button. Relevant API calls in UI objects that return a user's input value or listen to user's action/event are defined as triggers.

The anomaly detection in UTD is based on analyzing unauthorized privileged operations that are not intended by the user. Because the analysis is automated (i.e., without any user participation), user-intention needs to be approximated. In this analysis user-intention is embodied in the trigger variables. The authors specify the names of functions corresponding to triggers and operations in the program analysis.

A valid dependence path is a (directed) dependence path between a trigger and an operation in a data dependence graph (DDG) [78]. The path specifies a definition-and-consumption (*def-use*) relation, where a trigger is defined and later used as an argument to an operation. The existence of a valid dependence path means that the operation depends on a user trigger. The trigger may be transformed before being used as an argument in the operation, thus the dependence path between them may be long. (Figure 4 in [78] gives an illustration of dependence paths.)

A valid call site s of an operation c is a call site that has a valid user-trigger dependence path [78]. A call site is the occurrence of an operation. An operation may have one or more call sites in a program. UTD computes an assurance score V that is a single value for an app representing the portion of call sites that are intended by the user across all operations in the app.

The authors evaluated 2,684 free popular apps on Google Play Market and 1,433 malicious apps [78]. Their results suggested that this anomaly detection approach with the single feature of user-trigger dependence is surprisingly effective. It detects 97.9% of the malware apps with a low 2.0% false positive rate. The analysis also reveals hundreds of malicious apps in the Google Play market, some of which were previously unreported and were not detected by any of the (48) VirusTotal scanners.

UTD discovered a number of new malware apps. For example, UTD detected a malicious app `Time Machine`, which is repackaged from an ebook app. The malware invokes many sensitive APIs (in `Jslibs` library) to perform unjustified operations, such as recording sound, retrieving phone state, and exfiltrating geolocation information. Another malware is an organizer app `com.via3apps.usobesit618`. It is bundled with a piece of malware collecting private information, such as device ID, email address, latitude and longitude, phone number, and username. This app uploads the details to a remote server. Another malware detected is a game-guide app `com.bfrs.krokr`, which is bundled with adware `AndroidApperhand` (aka `Android.Counterclank`). `AndroidApperhand` is a piece of aggressive adware. It attempts to modify the browser's home page, copy bookmarks on the device, shortcuts, push notifications, and steal build information (brand, device, manufacturer, model). This adware also attempts to connect to a remote host.

For the apps that are labeled as malicious by only one rule (2.4% out of 2,684 apps), the authors confirmed that most of the apps (2.2% out of the 2.4%) contain aggressive advertisement libraries, such as `Mobclix`, `Tapjoy`, and `Waps`. These libraries invoke sensitive operations without any user triggers. Unlike regular ad libraries, these aggressive ad libraries contain an overwhelming amount of invalid call sites. Most of them have a large number ($> 50\%$) of sensitive operations with zero valid call sites, which is consistent with known malware.

4.4   FORMAL LANGUAGE MODEL FOR ANOMALY DETECTION

Static program analysis helps mitigate the incompleteness of dynamic program traces when modeling program behaviors. However, static analysis alone may not accurately characterize program behaviors in the real world. This section discusses the differences and connections between static and dynamic program analysis in program anomaly detection. Because of our focus on data-driven anomaly detection in this book, our description in this section is brief and we refer the interested readers to the full paper by Shu et al. [251]. Shu et al.'s work connects anomaly detection with the formal language and automaton theory.

Using a Turing machine, we explain the power and limitation of static program analysis in modeling program behaviors. Considering a Turing machine as the model for program execution. One can map each process (an executing program) onto the Turing machine. The machine code (binary executable) constructs the table of instructions, and the program trace is the tape at a given time. The table of instructions and a specific input determine the computation[2]—the tape at any given time. In other words, given the binary executable and the input, one is able to calculate the dynamic program trace and the corresponding program behavior.

While the static program analysis is powerful in theory, obtaining program trace using static analysis is expensive. The most precise calculation, i.e., symbolic execution, needs to simulate a random-access machine (RAM) for executing a program. It is possible to test one execution path at a time. However, the complexity of analyzing all possible execution paths is exponential.

On the other hand, data-driven models are constructed with dynamic program traces that are obtained in concrete executions. They can capture dynamic characteristics of programs, e.g., frequency patterns. The NP-complete issue of symbolic execution is also avoided. However, the data incompleteness problem discussed in Section 4.1 emerges. Thus, bridging these different paradigms (as done by STILO [302, 304]) is promising for improving anomaly detection capabilities.

Next, we briefly discuss the design of program anomaly detection models with static analysis. Our description gives an intuitive summary of the formal framework presented in [251]. Let's first explain the term linear bounded automaton. Although computations are commonly modeled as Turing machines, program executions are less powerful than Turing machines. A Turing machine has an infinite tape, while every real-world program is limited by its physical memory size and its software-accessible memory boundary, e.g., 64-bit address space. The limited Turing machine with a finite tape is called linear bounded automaton. A program-behavior model may be viewed as a linear bounded automaton. Specifically, a program anomaly detection system can model program executions as a linear bounded automaton.

An anomaly detection model can utilize a context-sensitive language to describe program traces. However, context-sensitive languages are expensive to construct. As a result, the majority of program anomaly detection systems use context-free languages to model program behaviors. Using context-free languages simplifies the model of program executions, specifically from a linear bounded automaton to a push-down automaton or a non-state automaton. However, the imprecision introduced by the simplification leaves more room for attackers to launch mimicry attacks [251].

Static program analysis can be useful for building any formal language models. For example, STILO and STILO-context models in Section 4.2 are hidden Markov models, which describe program executions as specialized automata. The model initialized with static analysis gives improved precision and faster training. Also, for example, LAD in Chapter 3 can be viewed as a weak linear bounded automaton model. LAD initializes its matrices with the call graph in-

---

[2]We simplify the problem of computation to deterministic computation for easy understanding. Random algorithms require separate discussion.

formation learned from static program analysis. These demonstrations successfully integrated techniques from multiple domains to improve anomaly detection capabilities.

SUMMARY

In this chapter, we showed various ways that insights from code analysis can substantially improve data-driven anomaly detection. Code (binary or source) is usually available for analysis in most scenarios. However, interfacing data science with program analysis inevitably increases the complexity of design and deployment. Requiring a client (organization or individual) to perform all the setup, training, and maintenance in-house on its own may be unrealistic. An outsourced setting with a trustworthy anomaly-detection service provider in the cloud is more promising. Issues arise when a system runs proprietary code that cannot leave the organizational boundary.

CHAPTER 5

Anomaly Detection in Cyber-Physical Systems

In this chapter, we discuss the unique security challenges in cyber-physical systems (CPS) and highlight the event awareness enhancement for CPS anomaly detection [53]. We take the finite-state automaton (FSA) model as an instance, and present the event-aware FSA model, named eFSA, to detect stealthy anomalous CPS program behaviors particularly caused by data-oriented attacks.

5.1 CPS SECURITY CHALLENGES

Cyber-physical systems (CPS) consist of a tightly coupled integration of computational elements and physical components. The computational elements rely on sensors to monitor the physical environment and make control decisions to affect physical processes with feedback loops [242]. These systems are widely used to operate critical infrastructure assets, such as electric power grid, oil and natural gas distribution, industry automation, medical devices, automobile systems, and air traffic control [261].

CPS and IoT (Internet of Things) have significant overlaps. CPS emphasizes the tightly coupled integration of computational components and physical world, while IoT has an emphasis on the connection of things with networks. If an IoT system interacts with the physical world via sensors or actuators, then it can also be classified as a CPS.

5.1.1 BACKGROUND ON CPS

In many instances, a CPS can be modeled as an *event-driven* feedback control system [73]. *Events* are referred to as occurrences of interest that come through the cyber-physical observation process or emitted by other entities (e.g., the remote controller), and trigger the execution of corresponding control actions. The close interactions and feedback loops between the control program and physical environment place events as the major building blocks in CPS [272].

In the industrial control literature, CPSs may be referred to as Process Control Systems (PCS), Industrial Control Systems (ICS), Distributed Control Systems (DCS), or Supervisory Control and Data Acquisition (SCADA) systems [39].

Figure 5.1a illustrates an example of CPS—a power plant boiler [293]. In this example, coal is automatically transported into the boiler when the boiler's temperature exceeds a pre-specified threshold (i.e., an event happens), and the amount of coal to be transported also depends on the temperature value. The pressure measurement, which is proportional to the temperature, can affect the operation of steam valves. The system is composed of the following components: (1) the physical process including the coal conveyor belt and steam valves; (2) meters/sensors that measure the physical environment; (3) actuators that trigger physical changes in response to control commands; and (4) the control program (e.g., programmable logic controller) that takes sensory data as input and makes control decisions. The control program and the physical process communicate through sensors and actuators, where physical environments are sensed and events (e.g., events coming from the environment or emitted by other entities) of interest are detected, and then actuation tasks are executed through a set of actuators. Figure 5.1b shows an abstract view of the event-driven CPS architecture. Typically, control programs are running on CPS field devices, which are embedded computers situated in the field.

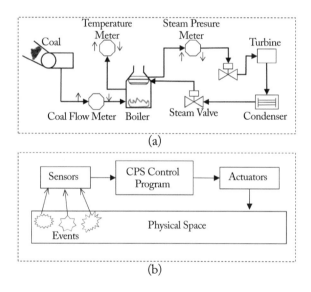

Figure 5.1: CPS background: (a) An example of power plant boiler; (b) An abstract view of event-driven CPS architecture.

5.1.2   SECURITY AND THE PHYSICAL WORLD

The tight coupling with physical space of CPS brings new security challenges. Traditionally, security was not taken into consideration in the design of many CPS applications, due to their isolation from potential attack sources. However, more and more CPS devices are connected to business networks and the Internet in the trend of IoT, e.g., the Internet-connected automobiles [47], making CPS increasingly vulnerable [232]. Though more connectivity improves efficiency and productivity in operations of physical assets, it significantly increases the number of access points to CPS, and thus more attack surfaces arise. Motivations behind CPS attacks include criminal attackers, politically-motivated espionage, and physical threats [133].

Unlike traditional security issues, attacks in CPS bring more serious damage due to close interactions between the control system and the physical world. For example, the Stuxnet [158] attack allows hackers to compromise the control system of a nuclear power plant and manipulate real-world equipment such as centrifuge rotor speeds, which can be very dangerous. In late 2014, a German steel mill was attacked, where hackers successfully took control of the production software and caused significant material damage to the site. More recently, attackers remotely controlled the SCADA distribution management system of Ukrainian Power Grid using the `BlackEnergy` malware. The blackout caused by the attack affected approximately 225,000 customers [83]. According to ICS-CERT's report [136], there have been increasing number of cyber attacks targeting critical infrastructure. Securing CPS against malicious attacks is of paramount importance for potential damages to physical systems.

Several studies [6, 48, 116, 327] have shown that embedded systems software running on CPS devices suffers from a variety of runtime attacks, including control-flow hijacking attacks (e.g., malicious code injection [94]), non-control data attacks [130], control-flow bending [41], and data-oriented programming [130]. These attacks can be broadly classified into two categories: *control-oriented attacks* and *data-oriented attacks*. The former exploits memory corruption vulnerabilities to divert a program's control flows. The latter manipulates data variables without violating the program's control-flow integrity. The majority of research efforts over the past decade have been focusing on control-flow integrity (CFI) [3, 5, 41, 95, 179]. Relatively little work has addressed the new data-oriented attacks.

Data-oriented attacks can potentially cause serious harm to physical systems, because many control decisions are made based on particular values of data variables in CPS programs. The threats are alarming. For example, data-oriented attacks in CPS may corrupt critical variables at runtime to manipulate control operations (e.g., impacting the number of iterations of a loop [6]), or execute a valid-yet-unexpected control-flow path.

Defending against data-oriented attacks in CPS is challenging, as they do not incur illegal control flows and evade all control-flow integrity based detections [130]. More importantly, CPS programs normally rely on external sensor events to make control decisions; this physical-event-driven nature makes it difficult to predict runtime program behaviors in CPS. In addition, this physical-event-driven nature of CPS also exposes control programs to various new attack surfaces, e.g., data injection and event spoofing attacks.

Fortunately, this intrinsic cyber-physical dependence also provides a channel for defenders to detect CPS anomalies. In order to achieve an attack goal, it is likely that a CPS attack would cause abnormal effects on the physical world. Thus, one can leverage the physical consequences of control actions to prevent cyber-physical attacks.

5.2   OVERVIEW OF CPS ANOMALY DETECTION

Due to the diversity of CPS applications, existing anomaly detection solutions are proposed to detect specific attacks for specific applications, such as smart infrastructures [261], unmanned aerial vehicles [193], medical devices [192], automotive [55, 230], industrial control process [39, 188, 282]. The majority research efforts on CPS anomaly detection can be generally classified into three categories: (1) cyber model (e.g., program behavior model, network traffic analysis, or timing analysis); (2) physical model (e.g., range-based model or physical laws); and (3) cyber-physical model (e.g., eFSA [53]). Table 5.1 compares representative CPS anomaly detection solutions.

Table 5.1: Representative CPS anomaly detection approaches

Research Work	Category	Approach	Security Guarantee	Validation
C-FLAT [6]	Program behavior model (cyber)	Program analysis and instrumentation	Control-oriented attacks and limited non-control-data attacks	Raspberry Pi testbed
Yoon et al. [313]	Program behavior model (cyber)	Syscall frequencies	Frequency-based program control flow anomaly	Raspberry Pi testbed
Feng et al. [82]	Network traffic analysis (cyber)	Machine learning based traffic analysis	Traffic alteration	Traffic data from a gas pipeline system
Zimmer et al. [327]	Timing analysis model (cyber)	Static/dynamic timing analysis	Code injection attacks	Simulation/Testbed
Hadziosmanovic et al. [116]	Range-based model (physical)	Attribute values extracted from network traffic	False data injection attacks	Traffic data from water treatment plants
Cardenas et al. [38]	Physical laws	Linear model derived from training data	False data injection attacks	Simulation
SRID [293]	Physical laws	Correlation analysis of system variables	False data injection attacks	Simulation
C2[186]	Control policies (physical)	User specfied control policies	Control signal violation	Raspberry Pi testbed
eFSA [52]	Cyber-physical model	Event-aware finite-state automaton (FSA)	Data-oriented attacks	Raspberry Pi testbed

- *Program behavior model.* Regarding the CPS anomaly detection based on program behavior models in the cyber domain, Yoon et al. [313] proposed a lightweight method for detecting anomalous executions using the distribution of system call frequencies. The frequencies are for individual system calls, i.e., 1-grams. The authors in [3] proposed a hardware based approach for control-flow graph (CFG) validation in runtime embedded systems. McLaughlin et al. [188] presented the Trusted Safety Verifier (TSV) to verify safety-critical code executed on programmable controllers, such as checking safety properties like range violations and interlocks of programmable logic controller (PLC) programs. Abera et al. proposed the C-FLAT [6], a technique for remote attestation of the execution path of an application running on an embedded device. In C-FLAT, given an aggregated authenticator (i.e., fingerprint) of the program's control flow computed by the prover, the verifier is able to trace the exact execution path and thus can determine whether application's control flow has been compromised. As explained in [53], C-FLAT only offers limited protection against data-oriented attacks.

- *Traffic-based model.* Control systems exhibit relatively simpler network dynamics compared with traditional IT systems, e.g., fixed network topology, regular communication patterns, and a limited number of communication protocols. As a result, implementing network-based anomaly detection systems would be easier than traditional mechanisms. Feng et al. [83] presented an anomaly detection method for ICS by taking advantage of the predictable and regular nature of communication patterns that exist between field devices in ICS networks. In the training phase, a base-line signature database for general packages is constructed. In the monitoring phase, the authors utilize Long Short-Term Memory (LSTM) network based softmax classifier to predict the most likely package signatures that are likely to occur given previously seen package traffic. The time-series level anomaly detector captures traffic anomalies if a package's signature is not within the predicted top k most probable signatures according to the LSTM-based model.

- *Timing-based model.* Several studies utilized timing information as a side channel to detect malicious intrusions. The rationale is that execution timing information is considered an important constraint for real-time CPS applications, and mimicking timing is more difficult than mimicking the execution sequence. To this end, Zimmer et al. [327] used the worst-case execution time (WCET) obtained through static analysis to detect code injection attacks in CPS. Such timing-based detection technique is realized by instrumenting checkpoints within real-time applications. Sibin et al. [194] focused on detecting intrusions in real-time control systems. Yoon et al. [312] presented SecureCore, a multicore architecture using the timing distribution property of each code block to detect malicious activities in real-time embedded system. Lu et al. [179] investigated how to reduce timing checkpoints without sacrificing detection accuracy in embedded systems.

- *Range based model.* Enforcing data ranges is the simplest method to detect CPS anomalies in the physical domain. As long as sensor readings are outside a pre-specified normal range, the anomaly detector raises an alarm. Hadziosmanovic et al. [117] presented a nonobtrusive security monitoring system by deriving models for programmable logic controller (PLC) variables from network packets as the basis for assessing CPS behaviors. For constant and attribute series, the proposed detection approach raises an alert if a value reaches outside of the enumeration set. However, range-based detection suffers from a low detection rate because it neglects the program's execution context, e.g., if the legal measurement covers a large range of sensor values, attacks can easily evade its detection.

- *Physical laws.* This approach requires system states in CPS to follow immutable laws of physics (e.g., [282]). Wang et al. [293] derived a graph model to defeat false data injection attacks in SCADA system. It captures internal relations among system variables and physical states. Cho et al. [55] presented a brake anomaly detection system, which compares the brake data with the norm model to detect any vehicle misbehavior (e.g., due to software bugs or hardware glitches) in the Brake-by-Wire system. Based on the prediction models and predefined threat constraints, these methods check whether sensor readings are consistent with the expected behaviors of a control system. Cardenas et al. [39] proposed a physical model based detection method by monitoring the physical system under control, and the sensor and actuator values. The authors also proposed automatic response mechanisms by estimating the system states. Urbina et al. [282] discussed the limitations of existing physics-based attack detection approaches, i.e., they cannot limit the impact of stealthy attacks. The authors proposed a metric to measure the impact of stealthy attacks and to study the effectiveness of physics-based detection.

- *Control policies.* Physical model can also be specified by control policies. The main purpose of the policies is to improve the survivability of control systems, i.e., without losing critical functions under attacks. For example, McLaughlin et al. [187] introduced a policy enforcement for governing the usage of CPS devices, which checks whether the policy allows an operation depending on the state of the plant around the time the operation was issued. The policies specify what behaviors should be allowed to ensure the safety of physical machinery and assets.

- *Cyber-physical model.* Such a model analyzes both the cyber and physical properties of CPS, as well as their interactions. It captures the cyber-physical context dependency of control programs. Thus, it is able to detect inconsistencies between the physical context and program execution. Cheng et al. gave the first such demonstration [53]. Their work, *e*FSA, characterizes control-program behavior with respect to events. They showed how *event-aware anomaly detection* defends against data-oriented attacks. *e*FSA enforces the runtime consistency among control decisions, values of data variables in control programs, and the physical environments.

As shown in Table 5.1, cyber models and physical models have different security guarantees. The former targets at detecting CPS control program anomalies in the cyber domain. While the latter mainly focuses on detecting false data injection attacks in the physical domain [175]. The cyber-physical interaction (i.e., interactions between cyber components and physical components) in CPS makes it difficult to predict runtime program behaviors through static analysis of the program code or model training. As pointed out by Cheng et al. [53], existing cyber models [6, 313] are effective against control-oriented attacks, however, insufficient to detect data-oriented attacks. An effective CPS program anomaly detection needs to reason about program behaviors with respect to cyber-physical interactions, e.g., *the decision of opening a valve has to be made based on the current water level of the tank.*

In the rest of this chapter, we describe a recent CPS anomaly detection work EAD [53]. EAD's program-behavior modeling is unique, as it is positioned at the interface between the control programs and the physical world. The threat model in EAD is focused on data-oriented attacks. Control-flow anomalies in CPS can be detected by conventional solutions as presented in Chapter 3, and are not discussed in this chapter.

5.3   EVENT-AWARE ANOMALY DETECTION (EAD) FRAMEWORK

In this section, we focus on explaining the new event-related detection capabilities offered by EAD, specifically how to reason about cyber-physical execution semantics of a control program in EAD. We also give examples of new data-oriented threats in CPS.

5.3.1   DATA-ORIENTED ATTACKS ON CPS

Data-oriented attacks on CPS may result in inconsistencies between the physical context and program execution, where executed control-flow paths do not correspond to the observation in the physical environment. We illustrate the new threats using a smart syringe pump example in Figure 5.2. The control program reads external input via the serial port, and the input triggers the syringe pump to pull or push a certain quantity of fluid. It is important to guarantee the control system operates correctly given its intended chemical or biomedical usage. However, a data-oriented attack in Figure 5.2a may trigger the `push-syringe` or `pull-syringe`, even though no movement (i.e., the external event) has been recorded, e.g., by corrupting data variables in a vulnerable function (e.g., in lines 3 and 5). The attack leads to unintended-but-valid control flows. An attack in Figure 5.2b may corrupt a local state variable (e.g., `steps` in line 10) that controls the amount of liquid to dispense by the pump. Such an attack may cause the syringe to overpump than what is necessary for the physical environment.

Without loss of generality, EAD [53] defines two types of events in control programs: (i) binary events and (ii) non-binary events. Binary events return either `True` or `False`, which are defined in terms of pre-specified status changes of physical environments and provide

```
① while(…) {                    ⑨ push-syringe(){
②   eventRead();                ⑩⚡ steps= … ;
③⚡  if(Push_Event())           ⑪   for(i=0; i<steps;i++)
④      push-syringe();          ⑫   {
⑤⚡  else if (Pull_Event())     ⑬     write(i2c,…);
⑥      pull-syringe();          ⑭     …
⑦   …                           ⑮   }
⑧ }                             ⑯ }
```

(a)   (b)

Figure 5.2: Two examples of data-oriented software exploits in a control program. An attacker could purposely (a) trigger control actions by manipulating the return value of Push_Event or Pull_Event, and (b) manipulate the number of loop iterations in push-syringe without violating the control program's CFG.

notifications to the control program (e.g., Push_Event or Pull_Event in Figure 5.2). Such events are commonly pre-defined and used in IoT's trigger-action programming ("if, then") model [146, 281]. Non-binary events correspond to the sensor-driven control actions within a for/while loop, e.g., values affecting the amount of control operations of push-syringe in Figure 5.2.

We categorize data-oriented attacks against CPS control programs into two distinct types, control-branch attack and control-intensity attack.

- *Control-branch attacks* hijack values of binary events in conditional branches to corrupt critical decision making variables at runtime to execute valid-yet-unexpected control-flow paths. For example, the attack may allow liquid to flow into a tank despite it is full [8], or prevent a blast furnace from being shut down properly, as in the recent German steel mill attack [105]).

- *Control-intensity attacks* hijack for/while loops of non-binary events to corrupt sensor data variables to manipulate the amount of control operations. For example, the attack may affect the number of loop iterations to dispense too much drug [6].

Unfortunately, existing program anomaly detection techniques cannot detect these attacks, as the detection does not incorporate events and cannot reason about program behaviors with respect to physical environments. Range-based anomaly detection (i.e., sensor readings outside a pre-specified normal range are considered abnormal [117]) would not work, as the overwritten variable may still be within the permitted range. C-FLAT [6], which is based on the attestation of control flows and a finite number of permitted execution patterns, cannot fully detect these attacks. Similarly, recent frequency- and co-occurrence-based anomaly detection approaches (e.g., global anomaly detection [249] and system-call frequency distribution (SCFD) [313]) cannot detect either type of the attacks, since their analyses do not model runtime cyber-physical context dependencies. EAD [53] reasons about control programs' behaviors with regard to physical environments, and can detect both types of attacks, including compromised for/while-loops or conditional branches.

Threat Model. EAD makes the following security assumptions.

- *Capabilities of the adversary.* EAD assumes that the adversary has successfully authenticated CPS field devices (or the control center) under her control to the local network, and is able to launch runtime software exploits which may be unknown or known but unpatched at the time of insertion. To an attacker's benefit, she is also able to be in the proximity of the victim devices when applying a sensor or command spoofing attack.

- *CPS platform.* It is assumed that the initial state (i.e., the training stage) of the application is trustworthy, which is a general requirement of most behavior-based intrusion detection systems. EAD also assumes the runtime monitoring module is trusted and cannot be disabled or modified. This assumption is reasonable, as it can be achieved by isolating the monitoring module from the untrusted target program with hardware security support, such as Intel's TrustLite or ARM's TrustZone [6]. At the time of detection, the user space is partially or fully compromised, but the operating system space has not been fully penetrated yet, and thus it is still trusted [327].

EAD focuses on runtime data-oriented attacks that involve changes of program behavior. Its prototype inspects system-call usage, but the approach can be generalized to low-level traces (e.g., instructions [200]). Other data-related attacks that do not affect observable program behavior patterns (e.g., modification of non-decision making variables) are beyond its scope.

EAD's security depends on that the observed events (used for detection) are real, not spoofed, or tampered with. There are multiple approaches for validating events, e.g., distributed event verification, physical models [282] for water system [117], and power grid [175].

5.3.2 REASONING CYBER-PHYSICAL EXECUTION SEMANTICS

There are four main steps in EAD's training phase. In step ①, EAD first identifies both binary events and non-binary events involved in the control program. In step ②, it performs the event dependence analysis to generate an *event-annotated CFG*, which identifies the instructions/statements associated with binary events, and control intensity loops associated with non-binary events. In step ③, EAD conducts the program behavior modeling, such as the HMM-based model [304], *n*-gram model [294], or control-flow integrity [5, 269], which is the basic model in EAD. The next step ④ is important. It augments the basic model with event constraints and obtains the event-aware program behavior model.

Steps ⑤ and ⑥ are the testing phase. In step ⑤, EAD monitors the CPS control program's execution and collects runtime traces. Whenever an event-dependent control-flow path is encountered in step ⑥, EAD checks the consistency between runtime behavior and program execution semantics, i.e., whether a specific physical event associated with this event-dependent state transition is observed in the physical domain. Figure 5.3 shows the workflow of EAD.

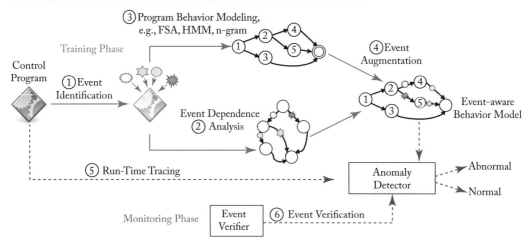

Figure 5.3: Workflow of the event-aware anomaly detection (EAD) framework.

Next, we describe the two key operations of *event identification* and *event dependence analysis*.

Event Identification

In order to discover the triggering relationship between the external events and internal program control flows, EAD first identifies what events are involved in a CPS control program. It is possible that events involved in programs are pre-defined in the library or event middleware. For example, ArduPilot [13] defines a set of built-in events for unmanned aerial vehicle platform. To facilitate efficient event-driven software development, middleware infrastructures for event handling are introduced. For example, IBM Watson IoT Platform publishes pre-defined events and other receivers that can subscribe to these events [295]. Identifying pre-defined events can be done through parsing the control program and is straightforward.

The main challenge is to identify (i) non-binary events and (ii) user-defined binary events. For non-binary events, one needs to identify a loop statement (e.g., for/while loop), in which sensor values impact the amount of control operations. To that end, EAD searches for all the loop statements that satisfy two criteria: (i) the loop is data-dependent on any sensor-reading APIs and (ii) there exists at least one actuation API that is control-dependent on this loop. This search is performed through backward data-dependence analysis and forward control-dependence analysis.

Identifying user-defined binary events is similar to the above process. An example of such an event is when the temperature exceeds a user-designated value, an event predicate returns `True`. EAD first searches for the conditional branch either `br` or `switch` instruction[1] without a

---

[1]LLVM intermediate representation (IR)

loop. Then, it performs the data/control-dependence analysis. Both the true and false branches of a br instruction are analyzed, as the branches may contain control actions or indicate implicit events. Event that are not happening can be considered as an implicit event.

EAD gives an LLVM-based event identification algorithm that automatically extracts these types of events. The extraction requires the knowledge of sensor-reading APIs and actuation APIs on the embedded system. The obtained sensor-reading APIs are *sources*, and the actuation APIs are *sinks* in the subsequent dependence analysis (described next).

Event-Dependence Analysis

The event-dependence analysis generates an event-annotated CFG to describe the set of statements/instructions that connect events and their triggered actions. Given an identified event in a control program, by conducting the forward inter-procedural control-dependence analysis, EAD identifies the statements that are dependent on the occurrence of the event. For example, given Push_Event() in Figure 5.4, the event-dependence analysis finds that push-syringe is control dependent on Push_Event(). It identifies the event-dependent statements, as depicted in gray in Figure 5.4.

```
① while(…) {                  ⑨ push-syringe(){
②    eventRead();             ⑩    steps= … ;
③    if(Push_Event())         ⑪    for(i=0; i<steps;i++)
④       push-syringe();       ⑫    {
⑤    else if (Pull_Event())   ⑬       write(i2c,…);
⑥       pull-syringe();       ⑭       …
⑦    …                        ⑮    }
⑧ }                           ⑯ }
         (a)                           (b)
```

Figure 5.4: Example of event-dependence analysis.

For the event-dependence analysis of non-binary events, EAD directly associates a non-binary event with its control-intensity loop. A challenge arises when dealing with nested binary events. EAD addresses this challenge using a bottom-up approach for recursive searching for event dependencies. Given a basic block that is triggered by a binary event, EAD backward traverses all the control dependent blocks until reaching the root, and extracts corresponding branch labels (i.e., True or False). Then, EAD transforms instruction-level event dependencies in LLVM IR to statement-level dependencies in source code with line numbers, which are the outputs of the event dependence analysis. In addition to static analysis, an alternative approach for event-dependence analysis is to use dynamic slicing [323], which can identify statements triggered by a particular event during multiple rounds of program executions.

5.4   EVENT-AWARE FINITE-STATE AUTOMATON FOR CPS

Many existing program behavior models, such as HMM [304], n-gram [294], or CFI [5, 269], can be augmented to realize the EAD framework and the event-aware capability. In this section, we present the event-aware finite-state automaton eFSA [53]. eFSA is an FSA-based instantiation of the EAD framework. In Section 5.6, we discuss the deployment challenges.

5.4.1   DEFINITION OF EFSA

eFSA expresses causal dependencies between physical events and program control flows. Without loss of generality, the eFSA model is defined as a six-tuple: $(S, \Sigma, s_0, F, E, \delta)$. S is a finite set of states which are PC values, and Σ is a finite set of system calls (i.e., input alphabet). s_0 is an initial state, and F is the set of final states. E represents a finite set of external events, which can affect the underlying execution of a CPS program. δ denotes the transition function mapping $S \times \Sigma \times E$ to S. Note that a state transition may come with multiple physical events. Thus, the input alphabet can be expressed as: $E = E_1 \times E_2 \times \cdots \times E_n$, where the input E consists of n concurrent physical events.

To avoid redundant checking, eFSA sets the checkpoint for a binary event at its first event-dependent state transition. For a non-binary event, eFSA performs the event checking after the execution exits the control-intensity loop.

Figure 5.5 shows an example of eFSA model corresponding to the FSA example in Figure 3.6 in Chapter 3, where an event dependent transition is labeled by "$[\frac{System\ Call}{PC}]$|Events," where | represents conditioning on and PC represents program counter. In this example, there are two binary events and one non-binary event. eFSA identifies binary-event dependent state transitions $[\frac{S_1}{3}\frac{S_2}{6}]|E_1$, $[\frac{S_1}{3}\frac{S_4}{9}]|\ \overline{E_1} \wedge E_2$, and a non-binary-event dependent control-intensity loop $[\frac{S_2}{6}\frac{S_3}{7}]|NB_1$. It also contains an implicit event dependent transition $[\frac{S_1}{3}\frac{S_5}{10}]|(\overline{E_1} \wedge \overline{E_2})$.

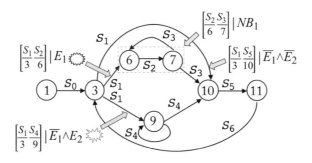

Figure 5.5: An example of the eFSA model [53].

5.4.2   EVENT-AWARE DETECTION IN *e*FSA

*e*FSA's detection involves multiple types of computation. The basic detection checks on the FSA state transitions, and more importantly the consistency between state transitions and physical events. They address the control-branch attacks (introduced in Section 5.3.1). These policies are straightforward to implement. An example of the control-branch detection is shown in Figure 5.7.

We highlight the *control-intensity analysis* that aims at defending against the control-intensity attacks described in Section 5.3.1. The analysis aims at ensuring that the control intensity is consistent with sensor measurements. *e*FSA first obtains the number of system calls invoked in each loop iteration, which is an invariant of the loop execution. Take Figure 5.5 for example. Each loop iteration in the non-binary-event dependent control intensity loop $[\frac{s_2}{6}\frac{s_3}{7}]$ always incurs two system calls. Then, *e*FSA models the relationship between sensor measurements and the amount of system-call invocations in a control intensity loop. Control-intensity analysis involves two operations as follows.

- *Execution Window Partitioning and Loop Detection:* Similar to LAD in Section 3.3.2, *e*FSA partitions infinite execution traces into a set of behavior instances based on the execution window. *e*FSA defines an execution window as one top-level loop iteration in a continuous program, and a behavior instance as the program activity within an execution window. Control programs monitor and control physical processes in a continuous manner, where the top-level component of a program is composed of an infinite loop. For instance, an Arduino program [12] normally consists of two functions called `setup()` and `loop()`, allowing a program consecutively controls the Arduino board after setting up initial values. The term execution window is equivalent to the *scan cycle* in industrial control domain [188].

- *Regression Analysis:* The purpose of regression analysis is to quantify the relationship between sensor measurements and the number of system-call invocations in a control intensity loop. By identifying non-binary events in Section 5.3.2, sensor types (i.e., sensor reading APIs) that are involved in a control-intensity loop can be obtained. In the training phase, *e*FSA collects normal program traces together with the corresponding sensor values. Then, *e*FSA performs regression analyses to model the relationship between the system-call invocations (i.e., outcome) and sensor measurements (i.e., explanatory variables) for each control intensity loop.

5.5   EVALUATION OF CONTROL-BRANCH AND CONTROL-INTENSITY DETECTION

The authors conducted two CPS case studies to experimentally demonstrate the detection of control-branch attacks and control-intensity attacks with *e*FSA [53]. We highlight the results in this section. The buffer-overflow vulnerabilities in the compromised control programs were artificially added to the otherwise secure code.

- *Syringe pump*,[2] an electro-mechanical device for dispensing/withdrawing precise quantities of liquid.

- *Solard*,[3] an open source controller for boiler and house heating system that runs on embedded devices.

Evaluation of Control-Intensity Anomaly Detection

In the syringe pump experiments, the humidity value determines the amount of liquid to be dispensed, which equals the humidity value subtracted by $30rH$. In the training phase, through control intensity analysis, the number of system calls with no event occurrences is 40 per scan cycle, and each loop iteration (i.e., dispensing a unit of liquid) in the control intensity loop corresponds to 3 system calls. The authors reproduced an attack that corrupted the humidity sensor value via a buffer overflow vulnerability, which enabled one to manipulate the movement of syringe pump [53].

Figure 5.6a shows the value changes of the humidity variable and the number of system-call invocations per scan cycle of the syringe pump. The normal humidity value fluctuates between $34\,rH$ and $38rH$. The amount of liquid to be dispensed changes accordingly. This amount is reflected by the number of system calls in each control loop. In the attack, the attacker manipulated the humidity values to be $20rH$ and $48rH$, respectively, via a buffer overflow vulnerability. *e*FSA recorded the number of system calls in each control loop and inferred the changes of the physical environment. This result is shown in Figure 5.6b. When the difference between the derived value and the sampled average value from event verifier was larger than $3rH$ (threshold), an anomaly was reported. Without the event handling mechanisms, none of these control-branch or control-intensity attacks would be detected.

Evaluation of Control-branch Anomaly Detection

When the temperature is lower than 50°C, Solard turns on the heater. When the temperature is higher than 60°C, where `CriticalTempsFound()` returns `True`, it turns off the heater. Through a compromised control program, the authors produced an attack that manipulated the temperature sensor values to be in the range of 40–45°C. This manipulation aimed to prevent the heater from being turned off properly. As shown in Figure 5.7, *e*FSA reported an anomaly at the first moment when it found an inconsistency between the execution semantics (i.e., temperature exceeding 60°C) and program behavior (i.e., heater turned on).[4]

5.6   DEPLOYMENT OF CPS ANOMALY DETECTION

In this section, we discuss the challenges associated with deploying anomaly detection solutions such as *e*FSA in CPS environments.

---

[2]https://github.com/control-flow-attestation/c-flat
[3]https://github.com/mrpetrov/solarmanpi
[4]The isolated dots in Figure 5.7 represent faulty sensor readings encountered in this experiment.

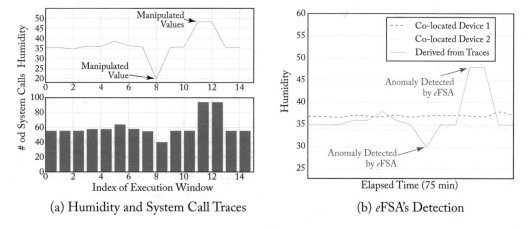

(a) Humidity and System Call Traces

(b) *e*FSA's Detection

Figure 5.6: An instance of the syringe pump experiments with a sampling rate of 5 min [53].

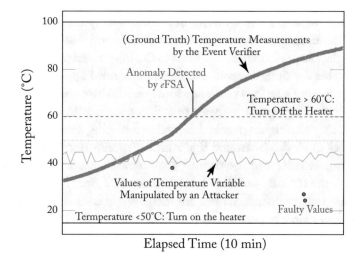

Figure 5.7: An instance of the Solard heater experiments [53].

Anomaly Detection as a Service: Embedded devices are resource-constrained compared with general-purpose computers. To reduce detection overhead, the anomaly detection may be performed at a remote server. EAD envisions the deployment to involve partnerships between hardware vendors and security service providers (similar to ZingBox IoT Guardian [328]), where the security provider is given access to embedded platforms and helps clients to diagnose/confirm violations. The client-server architecture resonates with the remote attestation in embedded systems, which detects whether a controller is behaving as expected [6, 283]. For detection overhead reduction, the remote server may choose when and how frequently to send assessment requests to a control program for anomaly detection. It is also possible to selectively verify a subset of events, e.g., only safety-critical events specified by developers are involved.

Bare-metal CPS Devices: *e*FSA works on the granularity of system calls and it leverages dynamic tracing facilities such as the `strace` tool, which requires the operating system support. An important reason behind the choice is that, the new generation of embedded control devices on the market usually come with operating systems [232, 269]. For example, Raspberry Pi devices with an embedded Linux OS have been used as field devices in different CPS applications [217]. Linux-based programmable logic controllers (PLCs) for industrial control have emerged to replace traditional PLCs [226] for deterministic logic execution. However, CPS devices may still operate in bare-metal mode [6], where *e*FSA cannot utilize existing tracing facilities to collect system call traces. For traditional PLCs, *e*FSA's security checking can be added to the program logic. The event checking idea can also be applied to an anomaly detection system at the level of instructions. It is possible to instrument the original control program with event checking hooks by rewriting its binary, e.g., inserting hooks at the entry of event-triggered basic blocks.

Tracing Overhead and Time Constraints: Although system call traces are a common type of audit data in anomaly detection systems, the conventional software-level system call tracing incurs unnegligible performance overhead to the monitored process [84]. The high overhead may be acceptable for time-insensitive embedded control applications, e.g., smart home automation, but would pose a serious challenge for time-sensitive applications. Existing studies commonly use the user-space `strace` software to collect system calls. For performance consideration, alternative tracing techniques may be adopted in replacing `strace` to improve the tracing performance. Pohlack et al. demonstrated that runtime monitoring of strict real-time systems is feasible, where functionality and monitoring requirements are known beforehand and predictable [218]. With the recently unveiled Intel's Processor Trace (PT) and ARM's CoreSight techniques, hardware tracing infrastructures are increasingly embedded in modern processors, which can achieve less than 5% performance overhead [284]. So, it is anticipated that future tracing overhead will be significantly reduced with hardware support.

SUMMARY

In the chapter, we explained the importance of event awareness in CPS anomaly detection. We showed how to reason about control-program semantics with respect to the physical environment. We gave specific examples (namely, EAD and *e*FSA) to demonstrate how to interface the cyber world and the physical world for security. We discussed their deployment challenges, including the advantages of deploying CPS anomaly detection as a service.

CHAPTER 6

Anomaly Detection on Network Traffic

Network traffic, including the headers, payloads, and traffic patterns, is an extremely rich source for anomaly detection. Network anomaly detection complements the system-level traces described in previous chapters. Vigna's overview of network intrusion detection research in 2010 pointed out the rise of anomaly-based detection on network traffic utilizing data mining [286]. PAYL [292] and McPAD [216] analyze n-grams with frequencies (described in Chapter 3) for modeling network payload in order to prevent server-side attacks. We have used PAYL's byte distribution analysis as an example to illustrate fine-grained modeling of normal behaviors in Section 3.1. McPAD utilizes an ensemble of one-class SVMs on network n-grams [216]. Wressnegger et al. gave a comprehensive treatment of n-gram based network anomaly detection literature [299]. Its suitability test is described in Section 3.1.3. An overview of anomaly-based network intrusion detection techniques can be found in [101].

In this chapter, we describe a new line of network anomaly detection research that aims to reason about network activities by modeling and enforcing their causal relations. These solutions include BINDER [69], multi-host causality [155], and Rippler [314]. We highlight the work of triggering relation graph (TRG) discovery. This causality-based anomaly-detection approach has been demonstrated to effectively screen HTTP and DNS requests from hosts [319, 320] and Android apps [321].

6.1 THREATS OF CLANDESTINE NETWORK ACTIVITIES

Advanced persistent threat (APT) describes stealthy and continuous hacking attempts targeting an organization or an individual, which may last for a long period of time without being detected. Determining whether or not networked hosts are infected with stealthy malware is technically challenging. The initial infection vector of most malware is usually through exploiting the vulnerabilities of common networked software, e.g., heap overflow vulnerability in web browser or its plug-ins. Once the infection is successful (e.g., zero-day exploits), network requests from advanced malware may not exhibit distinct communication patterns. For example, although virtually all malware activities require sending outbound network traffic from the infected machine, the traffic volume of stealthy malware may be low, rendering frequency-based statistical anomaly detection ineffective.

In addition, HTTP and DNS have been widely observed as the protocols for malware and botnet communications, as they are rarely blocked by firewalls [319]. DNS tunneling has been abused by botnets for command and control communications [301]. These abnormal outbound DNS queries are automatically generated by malware on the host, typically with the botnet-related payload. These surreptitious DNS activities are difficult to detect, because of their resemblance to regular DNS queries.

Such activities may be due to websites collecting sensitive user data, spyware exfiltrating sensitive information through outbound network traffic from the monitored host, bots' command-and-control traffic, and attack activities (e.g., spam or DoS traffic) originated from the monitored host. As malware tends to run as background precesses and thus does not receive any user input, by correlating outgoing network connections and processing information with user activities, one can capture malicious network activities. Legitimate DNS queries are usually issued by an application (e.g., browser) upon receiving certain user inputs (e.g., entering a URL into the address bar). The application then issues additional DNS or other requests (e.g., HTTP, FTP). In contrast, botnet DNS queries do not have any matching user triggers.

6.2   SENSEMAKING OF NETWORK TRAFFIC FOR ANOMALY DETECTION

Sensemaking refers to an analysis process including the tasks of investigating the complex data, exploring their connections, and gaining insights [81, 82]. Research also showed that higher-order information such as the underlying relations of events is useful for human experts' cognition and decision making (e.g., [115]). As isolated inspection of individual network requests is usually ineffective against APT, sensemaking for network security becomes a promising approach, e.g., organizing the otherwise flat and structureless network events into logically coherent structures, providing semantic interpretations to the vast amount of otherwise structureless and contextless network events. The rich structural and context-aware features can aid the sensemaking and the anomaly detection process.

For example, BINDER detects anomalous network activities through analyzing the correlation in traffic events by temporal (e.g., timestamps) and process information (e.g., process ID) [69]. King et al. includes the multi-host causality information in intrusion detection for dissecting attack sequences [155]. We give a brief overview of these solutions in this section. Then, in the next few sections we will give an in-depth description of the triggering-relation graph (TRG) work.

6.2.1   EXTRUSION DETECTION IN BINDER AND ITS GENERALIZATION

BINDER is the first work that exploits the connection between user inputs and outgoing network connections for security [68, 69]. It coined the phrase "extrusion detection." BINDER defines extrusions as stealthy malicious outgoing network activities, and points out that the key feature of extrusions is that they are not triggered by user input. In a later study, researchers refer to network requests without valid triggers as *vagabonds* [319].

BINDER is an anomaly detection method. It draws from empirical evidences a set of intuitive rules specifying how normal network events should be related. BINDER's rules emphasize on how normal network connections should be initiated and related. For example, BINDER defines parent-process rule and web-browser rule as follows.

- *BINDER parent-process rule:* A connection of a process may be triggered by a user input or data arrival event received by its parent process before it is created.

- *BINDER web-browser rule:* A connection of a web browser process may be triggered by a user input or data arrival event of other processes.

In BINDER, a user-input event includes the timestamp and the ID of the process that receives this user input. In comparison, the later TRG work includes more specific information such as input content or coordinates [319, 320, 321]. A data arrival event is reported when a TCP or UDP packet with non-empty payload is received.

The work in triggering relation discovery [319, 320, 321] generalizes BINDER for a much broader sensemaking effort. It detects anomalies by inferring the causality among network and system events. Triggering relations of events provide structural and logical interpretations to the behaviors of systems and networks. They illustrate why sequences of events occur and how they relate to each other, which helps reveal stealthy malware or exploit activities. The analysis in the context of underlying relations is more informed than examining individual events independently.

In the network literature, there has been a related series of research on understanding network application/service dependency for network stability and automatic manageability, e.g., Sherlock [17], Orion [51], and NSDMiner [197]. Rippler [314] proposed to actively perturb or delay traffic to understand the dependencies between service and devices. However, network sensemaking for security requires fine-grained request-level information. Thus, existing dependency analysis work at the network-service level (e.g., [17, 51, 197, 314]) cannot be directly used for network security. This finer granularity (requests as opposed to flows) demands different relation semantics and new scalable analysis methods.

The TRG-based anomaly detection is described further in the later sections. This sensemaking approach has been demonstrated for securing network traffic [319, 320], Android devices [321], and file systems [303].

6.2.2 MULTI-HOST CAUSALITY AND REASONING

Discovering causality among natural events (e.g., identifying factors in early childhood upbringing that may contribute to successful college admissions) has been studied by other disciplines such as economy and social sciences (e.g., [211]). The problem is difficult and requires complex probability analysis and statistical techniques. It is well known that correlation does not necessarily imply causality in general. For example, the positive correlation between drinking coffee and longevity does not necessarily mean longevity is a result of drinking a lot of coffee.

Unlike natural events, computer system and network events are artificial and man-made. In addition, the specifications on how these events should be generated and how systems interact and respond to each other are available and known. Therefore, unlike the causality of natural events, the causal relation inference is feasible and has been demonstrated (e.g., [155]).

King et al. demonstrated how to embed causality information in a backtracking system for multi-host threat reasoning and sensemaking [155]. The causal graphs span across multiple processes and hosts. They help eliminate unrelated events and alerts in intrusion detection. Causal graphs can be used to correlate alerts that may otherwise appear unrelated. Therefore, one advantage of this multi-host causality work is reducing false positives, supporting the triage and prioritization of alerts. That work gives examples of causal graphs for backtracking an email virus and correlating Snort IDS alerts [155]. The cost of the system is the process instrumentation and runtime overhead of all related processes in order to tag data and construct the causal graphs.

Another example of multi-host sensemaking work is HERCULE [213]. HERCULE targets enterprise-wide APTs, which usually consist of multiple stages and occur on multiple hosts in large networks. HERCULE aims to correlate events on different hosts and detects attacks across the network. HERCULE's sensemaking approach is unique in that it applies concepts of social network anomaly detection to network security. HERCULE first builds a "social network" on a vast number of log entries, according to connection rules. For example, log entries with similar timestamps and the same process ID are connected. This step produces a giant social network of logs. Then, HERCULE leverages community-discovery algorithms in Social Network Analysis (SNA) to detect APT attacks. HERCULE's detection is based on the observation that attacks are characterized by dense and heavy-weighted connections, whereas benign activities usually generate sparse and light-weighted connections in the log social network.

6.2.3   COLLABORATIVE SENSEMAKING

The cross-domain collaborative anomaly detection in AutoSense correlates web requests containing user submitted content across multiple web servers [25]. The cross-domain analysis is performed on requests that are deemed abnormal by local content anomaly detection (CAD) sensors. AutoSense detected application-specific attacks not belonging to an existing class of web attacks, as well as a wide-range of traditional classes of attacks including SQL injection, directory traversal, and code inclusion without using human specified knowledge or input. A key research question for cross-domain collaborative anomaly detection is privacy. AutoSense's solution is to use Bloom filters to store hashed n-grams. The only new information revealed is that the other site also has the same content, when a match occurs. Similar to other hash-based privacy-preserving solutions (e.g., [173, 176]), AutoSense assumes that brute-force attacks for inferring sensitive n-grams are out of its threat model.

For the evaluation, the authors of AutoSense measured the time gap between alerts across sites. Specifically, for the three servers in the evaluation, it measures the minimum time gap between alerts observed at one server and the same alert being observed at the other two servers. The result is visualized in Figure 6.1a [25]. The X-axis denotes the relative time elapsed since the start of observing the first alert. The Y-axis denotes the cluster. Each of the bars in the graph starts at the time when an alert is observed at a site and ends at a time when it is first seen among the other two sites. The observed large time gaps (e.g., hours or days) are desirable, as they give defenders sufficient time to take preventive action at the collaborating sites (e.g., exchanging blacklists).

Another experimental evaluation measures the reduction in the number of alerts. Figure 6.1b compares the number of unique alerts generated daily by the stand-alone CAD sensor and AutoSense [25]. The data includes both true positive and false positives. The X-axis denotes the time in one day bins and the Y-axis denotes the frequency of alerts observed on a log scale. For multiple sites collaborating, an alert needs to be seen at *all* sites. The authors observed an order of magnitude reduction in the number of alerts.

6.3   DEFINITION OF TRIGGERING-RELATION DISCOVERY

In this and the following sections, we describe the work on triggering-relation discovery (TRG) for network security. In the TRG model [319, 320], a *triggering relation* between event e_i and event e_j describes the temporal relation and causal relation between them, specifically e_i precedes e_j and e_i is the reason that directly causes e_j to occur. An event may be defined at any relevant type or granularity, including user actions (e.g., keyboard stroke, mouse click), machine behaviors (e.g., network request, function call, system call, file system access), and higher-level operations and missions (e.g., database access, obtaining Kerberos authorization, distributing video to select users).

Triggering relations of events may be represented in a directed graph—referred to as *triggering relation graph* (TRG), where each event is a node and a directed edge ($e_i \rightarrow e_j$) from e_i and to e_j represents the triggering relation. We also refer the triggering relation ($e_i \rightarrow e_j$) as the *parent-child* relation, where e_i is the parent trigger or parent and e_j is the child. A TRG provides a structural representation of triggering relations of observed events.

For specific types of network traffic, the TRG may manifest a unique topology and properties. We present one concrete example to demonstrate the triggering relations among HTTP and DNS requests in Figure 6.2. Suppose that a user clicks on a link to Financial Times (www.ft.com). The browser first resolves the IP address by sending out a DNS query. Corresponding HTTP requests are issued after the IP on address is known. Then, the user is directed

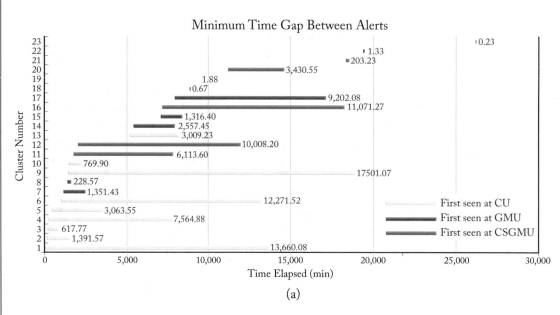

(a)

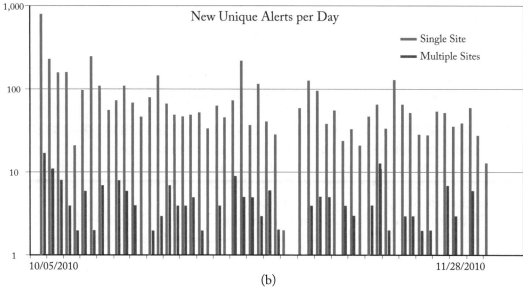

(b)

Figure 6.1: The time gap between alerts across sites in (a) and the reduced number of new un-labeled unique alerts per day that a human operator has to parse in (b) reported by the cross-domain collaborative anomaly detection work AutoSense [25].

to a news page by clicking on a link. The TRG forms a forest of trees that consists of user events and network requests. The user event of each tree in TRG is a *root trigger*.

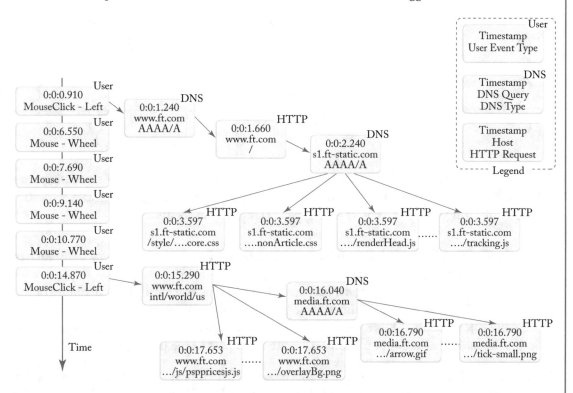

Figure 6.2: An example of triggering relation graph for outbound DNS and HTTP traffic on a host [320]. The network and user events are denoted as rounded squares. The arrows represent the triggering relations between events.

The problem of *triggering relation discovery* is that given a set of events, to construct the complete triggering relation graph corresponding to the events. The problem is illustrated in Figure 6.3. The problem of discovering triggering relations among a set of events can be transformed into the simpler problem of discovering the triggering relations of pairs of events, i.e., *pairwise* triggering relation. The next section describes a scalable machine-learning method to automatically predict pairwise triggering relations [319, 320].

6.4   DISCOVERY OF TRIGGERING-RELATION GRAPHS FOR HOST SECURITY

Discovering pairwise triggering relations is the key for recovering the complete network causal relations. We describe an efficient machine learing approach that extracts pairwise features for

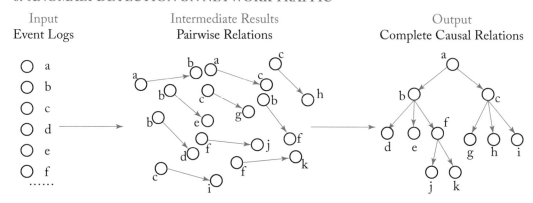

Figure 6.3: Given the individual network and user events as input (left), the problem of triggering relation discovery is to construct the corresponding triggering relation graph (right) [320]. The pairwise triggering relations (center) are a type of intermediate results.

binary classification [319, 320]. It is an anomaly detection approach, as the training only requires 1-class labeled data (i.e., normal traffic).

Pairwise attributes describe the differences of two events, specifically how attributes of the two events differ. It is formally defined later in this section. We first illustrate it in a simple example [319]. In Table 6.1, we show the attributes of three HTTP events. These attributes describe the individual network requests. They are the inputs to the pairing operation.

Table 6.1: Individual outgoing network events observed [319]. Time, Q Type, R Type, and ParentID stands for timestamp, request type, referrer type, and the ID of its parent event. The source IP of network events in this example is the same.

ID	Time	PID	DestAddr	Request(Q)	Host	Referrer(R)	Q Type	R Type
...								
4	22.723	2724	64.30.224.103:80	/	www.cnet.com/	N/A	website	NULL
5	22.733	2724	198.82.164.40:80	.../combined.js	i.i.com.com	www.cnet.com/	javascript	website
6	22.973	2724	198.82.164.40:80	.../matrix.css	i.i.com.com	www.cnet.com/	css	website
...								

There are three event pairs. Based on timestamps, we ignore the other pairs that cannot possibly have triggering relations. The pairwise attributes for each event pair are shown in Table 6.2. For example, the HostSim, ReferrerSim, and RequestSim give the similarity of two events in Host, Referrer, and Request attributes, respectively, according to certain similarity measures. The column Relation in Table 6.2 is what needs to be computed. Once computed, the binary value indicates the existence of a triggering relation in the event pair. For example, relation value of 1 for pair (4, 5) would indicate that event 4 triggers event 5, which is denoted by (4 → 5).

Table 6.2: Examples of event pairs and their pairwise attributes [319]. The last column is to be answered by the classifier, which predicts whether or not a triggering relation exists for each event pair based on the pairwise attributes. Q1 and R2 stand for the first event's request type and the second event's referrer type, respectively.

(ID1, ID2)	TimeDiff	PIDDiff	AddrDiff	Request-Sim	HostSim	Referrer-Sim	Q1	R2	Relation
(4, 5)	0.00	1	1111000001	1	0.5	0	website	website	**0 or 1?**
(4, 6)	0.25	1	1111000001	1	0.5	0	website	website	**0 or 1?**
(5, 6)	0.24	1	1111111111	0.1356	1	1	javascript	website	**0 or 1?**

The complete workflow of TRG discovery includes PAIRING, BINARY CLASSIFICATION, and TRG CONSTRUCTION, which is explained next.

- PAIRING is an operation that extracts pairwise features of event pairs. Its inputs are two events $e = (A_1, \ldots, A_m)$ and $e' = (A'_1, \ldots, A'_m)$. The output is the event pair (e, e') with m pairwise attribute values $(B_1, \ldots, B_m)$, where a pairwise attribute B_i ($i \in [1, m]$) represents the comparison result of attributes A_i and A'_i. That is, $B_i = f_i(A_i, A'_i)$, where $f_i()$ is a comparison function for the type of the i-th attribute in the events.

  The comparison function $f_i()$ (e.g., IsEqual, IsGreaterThan, WithinThreshold, IsSubstring, normalized edit distance, etc.) is chosen based on the type of attribute. Attributes may be of the following types: numeric attribute (e.g., timestamps), nominal attribute (e.g., file type, protocol type), string attribute (e.g., host name, referrer field, request URL), or composite attribute (e.g., four-octet IP address and an integer port number).

  Pairing is performed on *every two events* that *might* have the triggering relation. The pairwise features are used as inputs to the subsequent learning algorithms. Given a list of n network events, the total number of event-pair candidates is bounded by $O(n^2)$. To reduce the computational cost, one may pair up events that occur within a certain time frame, assuming that events occurring far apart are unlikely to have triggering relations.

- BINARY CLASSIFICATION is for a trained classifier to predict triggering relations on new event pairs $\mathbb{P} = \{(e_i, e_j)\}$. A binary label of 1 or 0 indicates the existence or non-existence of any triggering relation in an event pair, respectively. For example, $< (e, e'), 1 >$ represents that event e triggers e'. The classifier is trained with manually labeled training data.

- TRG CONSTRUCTION is the operation to build the complete triggering relation graph based on pairwise classification results. If event e_i triggers e_j in the event pairs $\mathbb{P}$, then e_i and e_j are connected by a directed edge in the TRG. Using the TRG construction to identify vagabond events (i.e., network events without proper root triggers) is straightforward.

For visualizing triggering relation graphs for human analysts, Zhang et al. summarized several usability requirements and proposed a compact radial layout [318]. How to better integrate human security analysts' effort in the anomaly detection process will be discussed along with other new research opportunities in Chapter 9.

6.5   SPARSITY OF TRIGGERING RELATIONS AND COST MATRIX

Due to the sparsity of triggering relations existing in network traffic, TRG leverages the customized cost matrices [79] to penalize missed relations during the training. In cost-sensitive classifiers, the cost matrix can be defined to weigh the false positive (FP) and false negative (FN) differently. A false negative refers to the failure to discover a triggering relation. A false positive means finding triggering relation in a non-related pair.

The cost-sensitive classification takes a cost matrix as an input. The trained model aims at minimizing the total penalty in imbalanced datasets. Due to the sparsity of triggering relations in network traffic, a cost matrix needs to penalize false negatives more than false positives.

Shown in Table 6.3, the cost matrix used in TRG is labeled by two categories: *with triggering relation* and *without triggering relation*. The values in the matrix are the weights for penalizing classification mistakes. Positive values are set for false negatives and false positives. For example, $\begin{bmatrix} 0,1 \\ 1,0 \end{bmatrix}$ is a cost matrix that has no bias on FPs and FNs; $\begin{bmatrix} 0,1 \\ 10,0 \end{bmatrix}$ penalizes the FNs 10 times more than FPs for a classifier.

Table 6.3: Semantics of values in a cost matrix used in TRG [320]

		Classified As	
		W/O TR	With TR
Ground Truth	W/O TR	TN: No penalty	FP: Penalty for finding triggering relations in non-related pairs
	With TR	FP: Penalty for failure to discover triggering relations	TP: No penalty

The use of cost matrix can have a significant impact on classifiers' performance. Figure 6.4 shows the accuracy of pairwise-triggering-relation classification and the correctness of root-trigger analysis under different settings (classifier and cost matrices) for the benign HTTP datasets evaluated in TRG [320].[1] The selection of the optimal cost matrix that gives the highest detection accuracy requires the trial and error.

---

[1]The HTTP dataset includes user events and benign outbound HTTP traffic in a user study with 20 participants. Each participant was asked to actively surf the web for 30 min on a computer equipped with the data collection program.

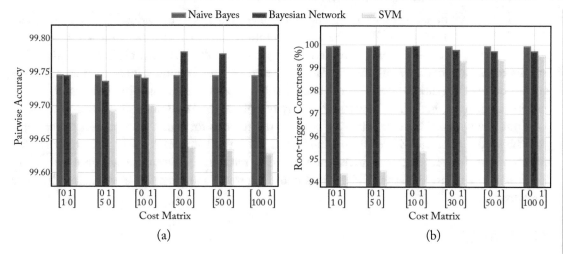

Figure 6.4: Pairwise classification accuracy and root-trigger prediction correctness results under various cost matrix conditions for a benign HTTP dataset [320]. The results of pairwise accuracy are shown in (a). The results of root-trigger correctness are shown in (b).

TRG defines the two metrics for evaluation. The *pairwise accuracy of classification* is the percentage of pairwise triggering relations that are predicted correctly by the classifiers. The pairwise accuracy is evaluated with respect to the manually confirmed ground truth. The *root-trigger correctness rate* is computed based on the root of a node. It is the percentage of events whose roots in the constructed TRG are correct with respect to the ground truth. The metrics allow the existence of one event having multiple paths to the same root in a TRG.
Sources of False Alerts. False alerts in TRG refer to benign network events that are misclassified as vagabonds. For the aforementioned HTTP dataset with a total of 45,988 outbound HTTP requests, the authors identify several categories of false alerts [320].

- Unconventional attribute values, e.g., requests to `googlesyndication.com` (for Google Map) usually have long referrers that the prototype does not expect.

- Requests sent out much later than their parent request trigger, e.g., requests for bookmark icons.

- Missing or incomplete attributes in the original data due to server configuration, e.g., redirection without properly setting the referrer field. There are 244 misconfigured requests that are sent to 38 different domains, usually image or video hosting websites.

- Automatic and periodic system and application updates that occur without user triggers. There are 157 update requests that are sent to 13 well-known legitimate domains. Whitelisting can be used to eliminate these alerts.

The TRG-based sensemaking approach has also been extended to Android platforms [321] and file systems [303]. The former solution aims to detect malicious Android apps, by constructing device-wide triggering relation graphs for all apps with HTTP activities. The graphs reveal vagabond events that are not triggered by user actions. The implementation requires rooting the Android device for data collection. The work addresses the new smartphone-specific challenges, including how to efficiently recognize the large number of automatic notifications and updates, missing attributes such as the referrer for traffic from non-browser apps, and the need for the host-wide monitoring [321]. The latter solution is on reasoning a host's file system events for security. It enforces the triggering relations between file system events (e.g., file creation) and user actions. The authors demonstrated its application in detecting drive-by downloads.

SUMMARY

In this chapter, we described several network anomaly detection methods that are all based on making sense of massive amounts of network traffic. Unfortunately, not all solutions that analyze network payloads work on end-to-end encrypted traffic. Thus, the detection, or at least the data collection, needs to be deployed at the edge of the network, e.g., on the end hosts or servers. This requirement may pose a challenge for outsourcing. In addition, the privacy risk associated with allowing service providers to access decrypted traffic needs to be addressed.

CHAPTER 7

Automation and Evaluation for Anomaly Detection Deployment

A key to deploying anomaly detection as a service is automation. Automation is necessary for virtually every step of the anomaly detection, including selecting detection algorithms, tracing and data collection, training, classification, and model adjustment. In comparison to anti-virus scanning, automating anomaly detection is much more challenging. A complete automation solution has not been demonstrated in the literature.

In this chapter, we discuss several issues related to anomaly detection deployment. First, we highlight some of the advances in automating anomaly detection systems. The automation discussion is focused on: (i) adaptive anomaly detection to capture model drifting [262], (ii) automatically sanitizing training data [64], and (iii) self calibration of anomaly detection models [66]. Second, we describe new advances in reducing tracing overhead. Tracing (i.e., logging system behaviors such as calls) has been a huge performance bottleneck hindering anomaly detection deployment. Intel Processor Trace (PT) is a relatively new hardware-based tracing mechanism, which was originally designed for instruction-level debugging. PT's fast tracing capability has the potential to bring anomaly detection deployment closer to reality. Third, we discuss the principles and methodologies for rigorously evaluating anomaly detection solutions. We point out the urgent need for anomaly detection benchmarks and standardized metrics.

7.1 MODEL DRIFT AND ADAPTING ANOMALY DETECTION TO CHANGES

The way users interact with complex modern systems often evolve over time, as can the systems themselves (e.g., patches). Consequently, anomaly detection models need to incorporate updates to their operating environment. Otherwise, the model may misclassify new patterns as malicious (a false positive) or assert that old or outdated patterns are normal (a false negative). This problem of *model drift* is a universally acknowledged hazard for anomaly detection deployment [262]. For example, in insider threat detection, a user's actions may gradually change over time [209], due to increasing skill or change in responsibility. A model which does not account for the drift would misclassify these benign changes as anomalous.

Model drift is also known as concept drift, usually in machine learning literature (e.g., [80]). Concept drift describes that statistical properties of target variables that a machine learning model tries to predict may have unforeseen changes. Researchers used an ensemble of classifiers with dynamically assigned weights to capture concept drift in data that may have slow, rapid, abrupt, gradual, local, global, cyclical, or other changes in distributions [80].

A straightforward solution for model drift is complete retraining, i.e., to rebuild the model from scratch in the new environment, including recollecting new traces and data and retraining the model. However, this approach is inefficient and time consuming, as pointed out by multiple groups of researchers [169, 262]. The long delay caused by data collection and retraining from scratch may be unacceptable for time-sensitive detection environments.

Updating the existing model with new changes is a much more efficient approach. For example, for adapting anomaly detection to software patches, Li, Gao, and Reiter performed binary difference analysis on the code before and after patching and designed algorithms with provably properties for updating detection models [169]. Stavrou et al. summarized the update requirements as follows [262]:

- identify and verify legitimate environment changes that pertain to the operation of anomaly detection sensors;

- update the normality model of the sensor in an efficient manner; and

- prevent the degradation of the anomaly detection model due to multiple or continuous changes.

In the rest of this section, we briefly describe the *spot retraining* proposal by Stavrou et al. [262]. It aims at altering the model only when there are possible legitimate changes in the modeled system behavior. In Section 7.3, we describe a different retraining approach called *gradual retraining* [66], which continuously updates the model.

The spot retraining approach assumes that security-critical patches only incur localized changes and do not widely perturb the model or constraints on data arguments. The authors first conducted a survey to gauge the impact that security patches make on program behaviors, such as control flow and data flow. The results are shown in Table 7.1. The Δs are computed by counting the number of control-flow changes, such as new control structures, new conditions, new functions, and new control transfers, as well as data-flow changes, such as new variables, new or changed arguments. Table 7.1 indicates that most security-critical patches enact small parts of an application's behavior model.

Using a SQL-and-HTTP setup, the authors then gave a specific spot-retraining demonstration [262]. The retraining is for updating n-gram based anomaly detection models (namely, Anagram [291] and PAYL [292]) of the web server, specifically on HTTP requests. What trigger the retraining process are SQL database changes or file system changes. For example, if a record is removed from the database, then the anomaly detection model for HTTP requests and replies needs to remove the information about the record in order to be consistent. Because of

Table 7.1: The size of a patch in lines (including comments), and the changes in data and control flow introduced by the patch of a vulnerability from [262]. The first column lists the vulnerable version of the application. These results suggest that patches introduce relatively confined impact to program behaviors.

Application	Patch Size (lines)	Control Flow Δ	Data Flow Δ
Linux-2.4.19	20	3	1
ghttpd-1.4	16	4	5
nullhttpd-0.5.0	12	2	1
stunnel-3.2.1	29	0	3
libpng-1.2.5	98	10	12
cvs-1.11.15	81	1	2
Apache-1.3.24	11	0	1
fetchmail-6.2.0	183	1	5
Samba (CVE-2004-0882)	65	0	7
Samba (CVE-2004-0930)	386	99	39
Firefox-2.0.0.3	22	8	0

the discrete nature of n-grams, updates can be effectively isolated and only have a local impact on the model (i.e., the set of normal n-grams).

Despite these advances, further research and development effort on this challenging topic is very much needed. Existing demonstrations are limited in the scope and scale. For example, spot retraining on statistical anomaly detection models (e.g., HMM) has not been demonstrated in the security literature [152, 304].

7.2   SANITIZING TRAINING DATA

For anomaly detection, the presence of an attack or anomaly in the training data poisons the normal model, which renders the system incapable of detecting future or closely related instances of this attack, producing false negatives. Taylor and Gates pointed out the lack of clean training data as a key roadblock to constructing anomaly detection models [103]. In this section, we describe a technique that sanitizes training data based on a voting mechanism [64].

7.2.1   OVERVIEW OF SANITIZATION APPROACHES

The solution, demonstrated by Cretu et al. in 2008 [64], has two types of setups: (i) a basic centralized setup, where the training data is collected from the same organization, and (ii) an advanced collaborative setup involving multiple organizations.

In the basic centralized solution, one first generates multiple models on small slices of the training data. These models are referred to as *micro-models* [64]. They are trained anomaly detection instances on small, disjoint subsets of the original traffic dataset. Each of these micro-models represents a localized view of the training data. Each micro-model is then used for the intermediate classification, which produces provisional labels for training inputs. Finally, the voting scheme combines the provisional labels of the micro-models to ultimately determine which parts of the training data may represent attacks. In the experiments, the authors generate micro-models from 3–5 hr of network packet traces, with the complete capture being approximately 500 hr.

This basic solution assumes that an attack or an abnormality appears only in small and relatively confined time intervals. Under this assumption, a training set spanning a sufficiently large time interval likely contains subsets of clean traces.

However, under advanced persistent threat (APT, defined in Section 1.3), this assumption no longer holds. Similar scenarios include that the training set may contain targeted attacks or there exist other anomalies that persist throughout the majority of the training set. To defend against such attacks, the authors proposed an improvement—a fully distributed collaborative sanitization strategy [64]. This strategy, referred to as *cross sanitization*, leverages the location diversity of collaborating sites to exchange information related to abnormal data that can be used to clean each site's training data set. The authors argue that although attacking all the collaborating sites is possible, it is considerably challenging, as the attacker will have to generate mimicry attacks against all collaborators and blend the attack traffic using the individual site's normal data models. This cross-sanitization strategy assumes the collaborating sites are trustworthy.

7.2.2   IMPACT OF BASIC SANITIZATION

Table 7.2 shows the impact of the basic sanitization on two *n*-gram based network anomaly detection models, namely Anagram [291] and PAYL [292]. The reported signal-to-noise ratios (i.e., TP/FP) are computed with or without the sanitization procedure, respectively. The experimental corpus consists of 500 hr of real network traffic from three different servers, www, www1, and lists. The first 300 hr of traffic was used to build the micro-models and the next 100 hr to generate the sanitized model. The remaining 100 hr of data was used for testing. The basic centralized sanitization setup is deployed.

These experiments show that the anomaly detection signal-to-noise ratio can be significantly increased, i.e., improved overall detection capability. There is one exception: Payl used on

Table 7.2: Impact of the sanitization phase on the AD performance [64], where A = Anagram; A − S = Anagram + Snort; A − SAN = Anagram + sanitization; P = Payl; P − SAN = Payl + sanitization. The values reported are signal-to-noise ratio defined as TP/FP; higher values mean better results.

Model	www1	www	lists
A	0	0	0
A-S	505	59.10	370.2
A-SAN	1,000	294.11	1,000
P	0	6.64	1.00
P-SAN	11.56	5.84	36.05

the www data set. In this case, the signal-to-noise ratio is slightly lower, but the true positive rate is still higher after using sanitization.[1]

The authors empirically identified a set of parameters that give the optimal detection performance, when using Anagram [291]. The parameters include the amount of traces for building micro-models, voting threshold, and weights of votes [64]. In addition, the authors also confirmed the detection of injected worms, including CodeRed, CodeRed II, WebDAV, and a worm that exploits the nsiislog.dll buffer overflow vulnerability (MS03-022). When trained with sanitized data, all instances of the injected malcode were recognized. That result suggests that the sanitization phase can both increase the probability of detecting a zero-day attack and previously seen malcode.

7.2.3 IMPACT OF COLLABORATIVE SANITIZATION

Another key demonstration is showing the impact of collaborative cross-sanitization, where the basic sanitization is crippled by APT-like attacks [64]. Specifically, after the basic sanitization, the anomaly detection model of an individual site may still be poisoned with attack traces. To isolate and remove these attack vectors, one needs to incorporate knowledge from other remote sources. This information sharing is the essence of cross-sanitization, which is comparing models of abnormality with those generated by other sites.

The sites share abnormal behavior characteristics, rather than their normal behavior characteristics. The reason is that normal behavior characteristics cannot be meaningfully shared because they are unique to an individual site. Individual sites can utilize external knowledge to cross-sanitize their training set and generate a better local normal model. The consistency of

---

[1]The true positive rate increases from 40–61%, and the false positive rate increases from 6.0–10.4% [64].

characteristics of abnormal packets across different sites can help filter out attacks that saturate the training data.[2]

In their experiments, the poisoned model refers to the setup where each of the three (3) hosts model is poisoned by each of the four (4) attacks (described in Section 7.2.2) present in the data. In their setup, when one site is poisoned, the other two sites are not. Every poisoned host receives the abnormal models of its peers in order to cross-sanitize its own poisoned model. Table 7.3 presents the average performance of the system before and after cross-sanitization when using direct and indirect model differencing (explained next).

Table 7.3: Performance when the sanitized model is poisoned and after it is cross-sanitized when using direct or indirect model differencing, respectively [64]

Model	www1		www		lists	
	FP(%)	TP(%)	FP(%)	TP(%)	FP(%)	TP(%)
Poisoned	0.10	44.94	0.27	51.78	0.25	47.53
Cross (direct)	0.24	100	0.71	100	0.48	100
Cross (indirect)	0.10	100	0.26	100	0.10	100

The model differencing operation supports sharing models of abnormal traffic among collaborating sites. Sharing these models enables a site to re-evaluate its local training data. The *direct* model differencing operation is for simple anomaly detection models that are comparable, e.g., sets. The *indirect* model differencing operation is for more complex probabilistic and statistical models. The indirect cross-sanitization reports consistent improvement on both the true positive and false positive rates. In the case of direct model differencing, once the cross-sanitization is done, the detection rate is improved, but the false positive rate degrades. The reason for this degradation is discussed next.

The authors measure the impact of cross-sanitization on the size of the models. The results are presented in Table 7.4, where *Abnormal* refers to the abnormal records that a site receives from its peers for cross-sanitizing its own model *Poisoned*. As Table 7.4 shows, model sizes substantially decrease after the direct cross-sanization for all three sites. This decrease leads to an increase in the false positive rate shown in Table 7.3. In comparison, the adjustment by the indirect cross-sanitization is more promising, as it boosts detection rates, without substantial model reduction.

In this section, the parameters used in the sanitization techniques are empirically determined, and the calibration has to involve human in the loop. In the next section, we discuss

---

[2]To alleviate the privacy concerns of sharing content, these models may incorporate privacy-preserving representations [173, 206, 207].

Table 7.4: The size of the sanitized model when poisoned and after cross-sanitization when using direct/indirect model differencing [64]

Model	www1		www		lists	
	# grams	File Size	# grams	File Size	# grams	File Size
Abnormal	2,289,888	47 M	199,011	3.9 M	6,025	114 K
Poisoned	1,160,235	23 M	1,270,009	24 M	43,768	830 K
Cross (direct)	1,095,458	21 M	1,225,829	24 M	37,113	701 K
Cross (indirect)	1,160,004	23 M	1,269,808	24 M	43,589	828 Kb

advances toward creating a fully automated protection mechanism that provides a high detection rate, while maintaining a low false positive rate, and also adapts to changes in the system's behavior.

7.3   SELF-CALIBRATION AND GRADUAL RETRAINING

A major hurdle in the deployment of anomaly detection systems is the calibration of these models to the protected site characteristics. Automatic self-calibration is important for the sustainability of operations. In this section, we highlight the self-calibration solution by Cretu et al., which uses only the intrinsic properties of existing behavioral data from the protected host [66]. Later in this section, we also show that the self-calibration technique can be used for gradual and online retraining [66], which reduces false alerts due to concept drifting. The authors built these solutions for network traffic based on the sanitization techniques in Section 7.2.

A naive approach for automatic parameter selection is to exhaustively try all possible value combinations, run the detection algorithms, and select the set of parameters that yields the best performance. A main issue such a mechanism has is inefficiency. Completing the full traing-and-testing cycle is quite time consuming. Thus, it may not give fast and efficient indication and feedback about the quality of parameters. The work described in this section solves this problem by specifying criteria or metrics that provide fast feedback to parameter selection.

The work in [66] aims to automate the selection of two parameters in the voting-based *n*-gram sanitization work of Section 7.2 [64]: (i) size of training data for micro-models and (ii) voting threshold.

7.3.1   AUTOMATIC TRAINING OPTIMIZATION

The size of training data for building micro-models is a key parameter in the voting-based sanitization work. Recall that a large training data set is partitioned into a number of smaller disjoint subsets (micro-datasets), each used for training a micro-model. Intuitively, choosing a smaller value confines the effect of an individual attack to a smaller neighborhood of micro-models. However, excessively small values can lead to under-trained models that also fail to capture the normal aspects of system behavior.

In [291], the authors define a criterion for selecting the training size parameter. It is based on the rate at which new content appears in the training data. Specifically, for a time window i, it computes the likelihood $L_i = \frac{r_i}{N_i}$, where r_i is the number of new unique n-grams in this time window and N_i is the total number of unique n-grams seem from the first time window.

The authors' experimental corpus consists of 500 hr of real network traffic from each of two servers, www1 and lists. www1 is a gateway to the homepages of students in the Computer Science Department at Columbia University running several dozen different scripts, while lists hosts the Computer Science Mailing Lists. The two servers exhibit different content, diversity, and volume of data. The data was partitioned into three separate sets: two used for training and one used for testing. The first 300 hr of traffic in each set was used to build micro-models.

Figure 7.1 shows the L values during the computation. At the end of the computation, an optimal training size is selected for each micro-model, with average value of around 2.5 hr.[3] The automatic selection aims at determining the stabilization point for which the number of new grams appears at a low rate (using a linear least squares (LLS) method for data fitting [291]). The authors compared the performance under automatically generated parameters with that under empirically determined parameters later in Figure 7.3.

7.3.2 AUTOMATIC THRESHOLD SELECTION

The selection of voting threshold is important for the micro-model based emsemble classification in [66]. A threshold of $V = 0$ is very restrictive; it means that a packet must be approved by *all* micro-models in order to be deemed normal. In contrast, a threshold of $V = 1$ is very relaxed; it means that a packet is deemed as normal, as long as it is accepted by at least one micro-model.

Similar to the previous parameter-selection problem, the key is to define a metric that efficiently measures the quality of a threshold. The authors define the optimal voting threshold V to be the one that provides the best separation between the normal data class and the abnormal class, which is intuitive. For a given threshold value V_i, one can define $P(V_i)$ as the number of packets deemed as normal by the classifier. One can normalize it and obtain $p(V) = \frac{P(V_i)-P(0)}{P(1)-P(0)}$.

The authors in [66] defined the separation problem as a constrained optimization problem, specifically to find the smallest threshold (i.e., minimize V) that captures as much normal data as possible (i.e., maximize $p(V)$). Therefore, if the function $p(V) - V$ exhibits a strong global maximum, these two classes can be separated effectively at the value that provides this maximum.

This method was applied to both the www1 and lists datasets, using Anagram. The profiles of both $p(V)$ (solid lines) and $p(V) - V$ (dotted lines) are shown in Figure 7.2. The value of V that maximizes $p(V) - V$ is labeled.

---

[3]We refer readers to Figure 2 in [66] for specific training-size values of micro-models.

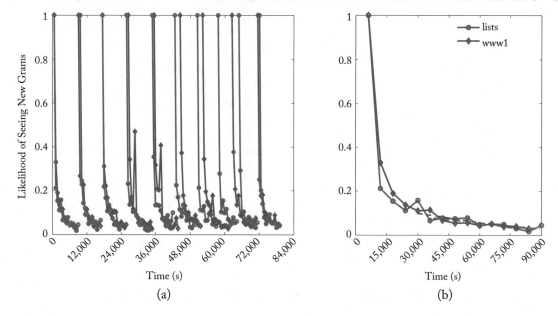

Figure 7.1: Automatic testing the parameter of the sizes of training data for micro-models from [66]. (a) Likelihoods L of seeing new 5-grams for 10 micro-models. (L value is reset after each training.) (b) Zoom on the first micro-model. The duration of a time window is set to 600 s.

7.3.3   PERFORMANCE UNDER SELF-CALIBRATION

In this section, we examine the quality of the models built using the automatically determined parameters, namely the micro-model training size in Section 7.3.1 and the voting threshold in Section 7.3.2. We compare their performance against the performance under empirically determined parameters. There is a fundamental difference between the two types of models. For the former, the sanitization process is completely hands-free, not requiring any human intervention. In contrast, for the latter, exhaustive human intervention is required.

Figure 7.3 presents the false positive and detection rates for models built using different sanitization parameters. The traffic contains instances of phpBB forum attacks (mirela, cbac, nikon, criman) for the host www1. The authors' experiments involve several configurations as follows.

1. *Both micro-model training size and voting threshold determined automatically.*

   The green star icons in Figure 7.3 mark the results of this fully automatic model. These fully automatically generated parameters give a 92.92% detection rate for www1, while exhibiting a low false positive rate of 0.16%. See also Table 7.5.

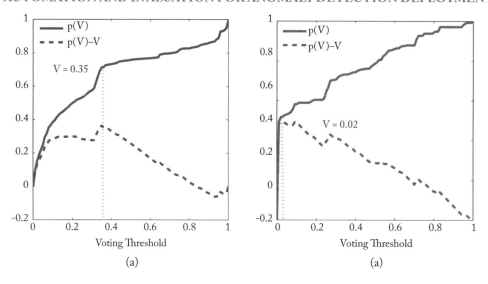

Figure 7.2: Determining the best voting threshold for (a) www1 and (b) lists [66].

2. *Automatically determined micro-model training size and fixed voting threshold.*

In the case of automated micro-model training size (the green line in Figure 7.3), the authors measured the performance of the models with fixed voting thresholds, ranging from 0–1, with a step of 0.1. In Figure 7.3, the models are capable of providing a high detection rate in the range of 94.94% and 92.92%, while maintaining a low false positive rate (< 0.17%).

3. *A fixed micro-model training size and automatically determined voting threshold.*

Empirical findings show that the micro-model training sizes of 1-, 3-, and 6-hr exhibit high performance for www1. For each of these values, the authors then analyzed the performance of the models built with an automatically determined voting threshold. Each line in Figure 7.3 with the color of pink, red, or blue represents a given training-size value. The triangular markers in the corresponding colors represent the results obtained with the automatically determined voting threshold. We can observe that the automatically chosen voting thresholds (colored triangles) are all placed in the safety zone, for which the 100% detection rate is maintained, while exhibiting a low false positive rate (< 0.17%).

Table 7.5 summarizes the values of false positive (FP) and true positive (TP) rates for the fully automated sanitized model, the empirical optimal sanitized model and the non-sanitized model, for both hosts www1 and lists. With automated parameters, for the host lists the automatic parameters achieve the same values as in the case of empirically determined parameters, while for www1 the values differ, but we observe that in the absence of the sanitization process

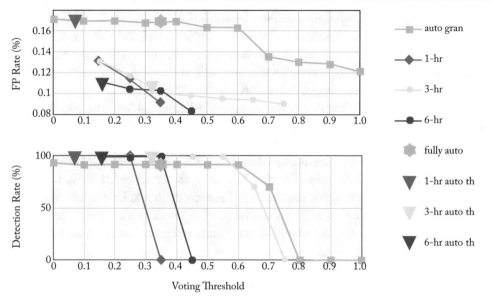

Figure 7.3: Model performance comparison for `www1` under automated or empirical parameters [66].

the detection rate would be 0. The key aspect is that the fully-automated sanitization still significantly improves the quality of the anomaly detection models while setting its parameters based only on the intrinsic characteristics of the data and without any user intervention.

Table 7.5: Empirically vs. automatically determined parameters for both hosts `www1` and `lists` [66]

Parameters	www1		lists	
	FP(%)	TP(%)	FP(%)	TP(%)
N/A (no sanitization)	0.07	0	0.04	0
Empirical	0.10	100	0.10	100
Fully Automated	0.16	92.92	0.10	100

7.3.4   GRADUAL RETRAINING

The ability of automatic parameter selection described in the previous section lends itself to a gradual retraining technique. In this section, we summarize the key findings on gradual retraining of n-gram based anomaly detection models (namely Anagram) with sanitization [66]. The authors tested their gradual retraining method for traffic from the same site, collected at months difference. Their comparison is performed between a static model and a dynamic model [66]. A static model does not employ any model update mechanism, i.e., the data sanitization model is built only once. A dynamic model changes continuously and has an online sanitization process. The related spot retraining technique is presented in Section 7.1.

A major challenge in retraining is that one cannot distinguish between a legitimate change and a long-lasting attack that slowly pollutes the majority of the micro-models [66]. A well-crafted attack can potentially introduce malicious changes at the same or even smaller rate of legitimate behavioral drift. As such, it cannot be distinguished using strictly introspective methods that examine the characteristics of traffic. However, the attacker has to be aware, guess, or brute-force the drift parameters to be successful with such an attack. In the previous Section 7.2, we point out a collaborative solution that can be used to break this dilemma. In what follows, we assume that all the changes in system behaviors are benign, i.e., long-lasting data-polluting attacks are out of the threat model.

When analyzing 500 hr of traffic data, the authors observed no significant difference between the alert rate exhibited by the static and dynamic models (Figure 9 in [66]). In terms of the detection accuracy, the authors obtained mixed results. Specifically, Table 7.6 presents both the false positive rate (including the binary packets) and the detection rate for hosts www1 and lists. For www1 the signal-to-noise ratio (i.e., TP/FP) is improved from 155.21 to 158.66, while for lists it decreases from 769.23 to 384.61.

Table 7.6: Static model vs. dynamic models alert rate [66]

Model	www1		lists	
	FP(%)	TP(%)	FP(%)	TP(%)
Static Model	0.61	94.68	0.13	100
Dynamic Models	0.62	98.37	0.26	100

The authors then investigated the concept drift appearing at a larger scale such as weeks and months, as opposed to days. They tested their method for traffic from the same site, collected at months difference. Figure 7.4 presents the alert rate for both static and dynamic models. Vertical lines mark the boundary between new and old traffic. One can observe that when changes happen in the system, the alert rate increases for both static and dynamic models. After the dynamic models start updating to the new data, there is a drop in the alert rate, back to levels below 1%. For the static model without retraining, the alert rate stays at about 7%. In the static model, spikes in the number of alerts due to concept drift can render manual processing difficult. These results indicate the retraining indeed successfully reduces the alert rate for a longer timespan.

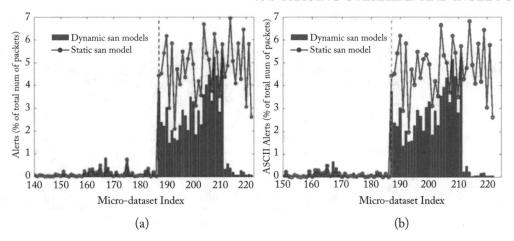

Figure 7.4: Automatic gradual retraining of the anomaly detection model for *www1*, in terms of alert rates for both binary and ASCII packets in (a) and ASCII packets only in (b) [66]. Vertical lines mark the boundary between new and old traffic.

7.4   TRACING OVERHEAD AND INTEL PT

Tracing has been a serious performance bottleneck for anomaly detection, hindering the deployment of this technology in practice. In this section, we experimentally compare the tracing overhead at various levels of a system, for both x86 and ARM devices. We also point out the potential impact of hardware-assisted instruction-level tracing such as Intel Processor Trace (PT) on anomaly detection deployment.

We measured the runtime performance overhead of different system call tracing tools on the desktop computer (Ubuntu 16.04, Intel Xeon processor 3.50 GHz and 16 GB of RAM), including PIN, SystemTap, strace. These tracing tools are widely used in anomaly detection (e.g., [249, 302, 304]), system diagnosis (e.g., [326]), and malware analysis (e.g., [183]). The programs and test cases used in the experiments include three utility applications (i.e., tcas, replace, schedule) from the Software-artifact Infrastructure Repository (SIR) benchmark suite [253]. SIR was also used in STILO [304] and STILO-context [302]. For both Tables 7.7 and 7.8, each number is averaged from thousands of testcases, specifically 5,472 test cases for replace, 2,650 test cases for schedule, and 1,608 test cases for tcas.

The tracing overhead on the Intel device is shown in Table 7.7. The baseline refers to the execution time of a program without running any tracing tool. SystemTap is a kernel instrumentation tool, and intercepts system calls in the form of a loadable kernel module. SystemTap's instrumentation incurs a low overhead with around 30% slowdown. The runtime performance overhead of strace shows around 2.5X slowdown. When printing call stacks on every sys-

Table 7.7: Tracing overhead on an x86 device

	Baseline	PIN	SystemTap	Strace	Strace w/Callstack
tcas	0.000018s	0.024063s (1336x)	0.000023s (1.28x)	0.000046s (2.56x)	0.000079s (4.49x)
replace	0.000066s	0.051280s (776x)	0.000079s (1.20x)	0.000155s (2.35x)	0.000256s (3.87x)
schedule	0.000073s	0.107846s (1477x)	0.000095s (1.30x)	0.000164s (2.25x)	0.000258s (3.53x)

tem call in `strace` (with stack unwinding support enabled), it incurs around 4X slowdown on average.

PIN is Intel's dynamic binary instrumentation framework that enables the creation of dynamic program analysis tools. We observe that `PIN` tool incurs a rather significant runtime overhead. This slowdown ranges from a factor of several hundreds to a factor of more than one thousand compared with the execution time of uninstrumented binary. In our experiments, we traced all system calls and their arguments, which inserts a checkpoint and analysis routine for every instruction. We need to insert the checkpoint at every instruction, in order to check whether the current instruction is a system call invocation. Our analysis routine logs trace to the disk, which incurs disk I/O. This high level of overhead observed is clearly problematic for deployment. PIN's overhead can vary significantly, depending on the instrumentation, specifically how much the instrumentation impacts the program execution. A better 2.7X slowdown has previously been reported for anomaly detection [249]. Cohn gave several practical suggestions to reduce PIN tool overhead [58], including to instrument at the largest granularity whenever possible, to shift computation from the analysis routine to the instrumentation routine whenever possible.

Table 7.8: Tracing overhead on a Raspberry Pi device

	Baseline	Strace	Strace w/Callstack
tcas	0.000757 s	0.001497s (1.97x)	0.001603s (2.12x)
replace	0.000717 s	0.001597s (2.23x)	0.001820s (2.53x)
schedule	0.001042 s	0.002131s (2.05x)	0.002200s (2.11x)

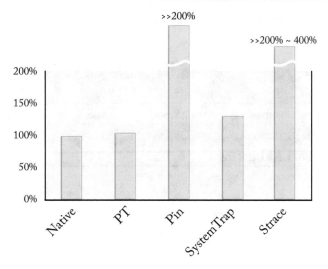

Figure 7.5: A comparison of various tracing mechanisms.

We also conducted similar tracing experiments on a Raspberry Pi device. The experimental results on Raspberry Pi 2 are reported in Table 7.8. It shows that the strace brings around 2X slowdown. The system call tracing overhead with stack unwinding only incurs a little higher overhead than the case without printing call stack.

The new Intel Processor Trace (PT) technology has the potential to bring anomaly detection to the wide deployment. PT provides fast hardware-assisted tracing with a low overhead around 5% [156]. As illustrated in Figure 7.5, this low overhead is a substantial improvement compared to existing methods. Fast instruction-level tracing by PT is a giant leap forward toward the reality of anomaly detection deployment. Instruction-level anomaly detection remains an interesting open research problem, which we will discuss in Chapter 9.

In addition, the recent work, Ninja, offers fast hardware-assisted tracing on ARM platforms (e.g., Raspberry Pi) [200]. The overhead of instruction tracing and system call tracing on CF benchmark are negligibly small. CF-Bench is for measuring both the Java performance and native performance in Android system. The results, conducted on a 64-bit ARMv8 Juno r1 board, are shown in Table 7.9. Similar low overhead for instruction and system call tracing was also observed for computation intensive applications (see Table 2 in [200]). In contrast, the high-level Android API tracing is slow.

Table 7.9: Ninja's tracing overhead on an ARM device with CF-Bench [200]. The numbers are scores output by running CF-Bench.

	Mean	STD	Slowdown
Base: Tracing disabled	25,380	1,023	N/A
Instruction tracing	25,364	908	1X
System call tracing	25,360	774	1X
Android API tracing	6,452	24	4X

7.5   EXPERIMENTAL EVALUATION FOR DATA-DRIVEN ANOMALY DETECTION

A precursor to anomaly detection deployment is the successful experimental evaluation of detection technologies in controlled lab environments. For data-driven anomaly detection, experiments are particularly important. Experiments need be scientific, rigorous, and complete. Oftentimes, security researchers need to set up experiments creatively. Halperin et al. famously used a bag containing bacon and ground beef to simulate the implantation of a pacemaker in a human for the security evaluation [119]. In this section, we discuss key challenges in anomaly detection evaluation.

Synthetic Anomalies and Attack Traces

As repetitively shown through examples in this book, detection accuracy including false positive and false negative rates is the first and foremost question to be evaluated through experiments. Both evaluations need to be performed side by side under the same detection configuration.

False negative evaluation is conducted on abnormal and attack traces, which can be synthesized or reproduced. Reproducing real-world attacks and demonstrating their detection are a key and necessary step in evaluating security guarantees. However, some attacks may be relatively easy to detect (e.g., invoking foreign system calls), as they are invented without the anomaly detection in mind. Therefore, it is important to be explicit about the attack capabilities and to validate them experimentally.

Synthetic anomaly traces have been used in multiple places to evaluate detection capabilities. For example, in both STILO [304] and STILO-context [302], synthetic abnormal segments of 15-call length were used. They were generated by replacing the last third of a normal call segment with randomly ordered calls from the legitimate call set. The call set consists of the distinct calls in a program's traces. The results are shown in Figure 7.6. Also for example, the LAD evaluation described in Section 3 included four types of synthetic anomalous matrices (Figure 5 in [250]).

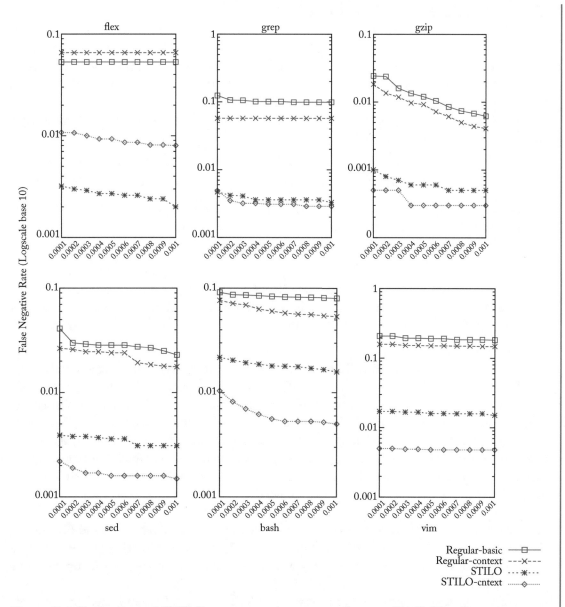

Figure 7.6: Evaluation of STILO-context with system call traces [302]. The figure compares 4 models, namely STILO-context, STILO, and Regular HMM (Regular-basic) and Regular HMM with context (Regular-context), in terms of false negative rates (in Y-axis, base 10 log scale) for Linux utility programs on system call traces under the same false positive rates (in X-axis). False negative experiments use synthetic traces.

Common Pitfalls in Anomaly Detection Evaluation

Drawing from our research and review experiences, we describe several common pitfalls in anomaly detection research, in particularly on experimental evaluation. The most common pitfall is focusing on explaining how to detect, but failing to explain why the work is important and why the detected anomalies are meaningful for security. In other words, the pitfall is not being able to properly state or demonstrate security applications.

The key fix for this weakness is to orient the evaluation design around demonstrating new security capabilities. Experimentally, it involves multiple components.

- One needs to reproduce attacks or anomalies in the threat model. It is important to map anomalies to potential attacks or real-world security problems, as explained in Chapter 2.

- One needs to compare the performance with state-of-the-art methods or some baselines. It means that (i) to demonstrate that existing state-of-the-art methods are inadequate against these threats, and (ii) to demonstrate the detection of these threats by the proposed technique.

- The evaluation needs to cover accuracy (including both false negative and false positive rates) and runtime performance. In addition, causes of missed detections and false alarms and other security limitations need to be investigated, which usually requires manual effort.

Tools, Benchmarks, and Datasets

In a recent effort toward building a foundation for unsupervised anomaly detection research, Goldstein and Uchida evaluated 19 different unsupervised anomaly detection algorithms on 10 different datasets from multiple application domains [111]. The authors published the source code and the datasets [110]. The work also summarizes the strengths and weaknesses of various approaches and the impact of parameter settings for local or global anomaly detection. The only security dataset is the KDD Cup '99 on intrusion detection, which is a version of the DARPA 1998 dataset (discussed below). In Chapter 9, we discuss how to generalize their work to a comprehensive anomaly detection knowledge base.

For program anomaly detection, the code and dataset for STILO and STILO-context (described in Chapter 4) anomaly detection can be found in [124]. An n-gram and FSA-based program anomaly detection lab can be found in [196, 247]. Tools for collecting system call traces and trace datasets including both benign and attack traces can be found in [34]. An open-source version of Anagram called *Salad* is available [298].

Several general-purpose outlier detection datasets exist. The Outlier Detection DataSets (ODDS) provide the access to a large collection of outlier detection datasets with ground truth [204]. ODDS include network security data, e.g., intrusion detection with DDoS attack scenarios. The supplementary material for the (unsupervised) outlier detection work [36] contains 20+ datasets, as well as the authors' outlier detection results [35].

A collection of publicly available PCAP files used for network-related cyber-defense exercises (CDX), malware detection, and forensics is maintained by NETRESEC [195]. It points to the USMA CDX dataset [278], which is described in [231]. Some datasets in the CAIDA collection [32] contain attack traffic (e.g., DDoS attacks). IDS datasets include Australian Defense Force Academy (ADFA) IDS Datasets [1], and University of New Mexico Intrusion Detection Dataset [279].

The HTTP requests and user events used in TRG for evaluating traffic causality (described in Chapter 6) can be obtained upon requests [43]. Glasser and Lindauer described methods to synthesize insider threat data that achieves a high level of human realism [38, 108]. Their insider threat test datasets are available [273]. Using an augmented version of the datasets, researchers conducted a large-scale insider threat detection in 2013 [237].

Network traffic datasets that are useful for false positive evaluation include the following. These datasets are assumed benign and free of abnormal activities. In addition, Perdisci maintained a list of security datasets and tools [215].

- Community Resource for Archiving Wireless Data At Dartmouth (CRAWDAD) dataset [33], which was used in [266] for false positive reduction evaluation.

- Enterprise Network Traffic Dataset from Lawrence Berkeley National Lab (LBNL)/International Computer Science Institute (ICSI) [159].

- Enterprise Network Traffic Dataset from a company called M57 Patents [180].

- Internet Traffic Archive (ITA) [134].

- RIPE Routing Information Service BGP Dataset [221].

The 1999 DARPA IDS dataset [171] has been used in many papers (e.g., [292]). Some researchers reported that the 1998 and 1999 DARPA IDS datasets are flawed and may not be suitable for experiments [186, 231].

Unfortunately, there seems to be no benchmark for anomaly detection evaluation. The community needs to publish benchmarks for various types of anomalies and attacks (e.g., local, global, ROP, or DOP) at different granularity (e.g., instructions, system calls, or library calls) or data types (network traffic or system traces). Benchmarks consisting of benign activities and concept drifts for false positive evaluation are also needed.

SUMMARY

In this chapter, we showed the technical advances in automating n-gram based detection. Automatic calibration, adjustment, and maintenance are the key to realizing anomaly detection as a security service and large-scale deployment. Supporting other complex algorithms, including global anomaly detection, needs to be done. Anomaly detection under adversarial machine learning [131, 277] is a topic that has not been explored. Under adversarial machine learning, an attacker may manipulate training data to compromise the classifiers. Whether or not the sanitization techniques presented in this chapter can be applied to mitigate adversarial machine learning is an open problem.

CHAPTER 8

Anomaly Detection from the Industry's Perspective

Anomaly detection is attractive in that the technology is not limited to existing knowledge of intrusions. However, practicality issues of anomaly detection algorithms and systems hinder the adoption in industry. Anomaly detection components in commercial security products are relatively new, which is in clear contrast with the much more mature signature-based intrusion detection technology. Today, researchers from both academia and industry work to overcome the challenges [265]. More and more security firms engage in developing anomaly detection systems against advanced stealthy attacks.

This chapter describes the core of today's most valuable cyber defense practices, in terms of infrastructure, organization, and utilities; how anomaly detection can be incorporated into the system; and what the available anomaly detection tools are.

8.1 ANOMALY DETECTION IN PAYMENT CARD INDUSTRY

Anomaly detection in the payment card industry is very successful. The security goal in a payment ecosystem is to find unauthorized transactions timely and accurately. Card organizations and their partners such as Visa, Xerox, and IBM have developed anomaly detection algorithms to profile users in terms of their spending habits and transaction relations, so that their system can identify anomalous transactions when a card is stolen. Some of the algorithms are further developed to capture frauds on the fly, or target specific stealth frauds such as "high-speed fraud" [141]. This specific fraud exploits slow detection mechanisms by conducting fraud activities in a short amount of time. The transactions themselves create an anomalous pattern, yet it is challenging to detect anomalous patterns, e.g., high-speed fraud, in real time.

For the fraud detection in credit/bank card transactions, false positives are still common. For example, according to a recent poll by `CreditCards.com`, among the people who have received fraud alerts from their banks, only 24% said the bank got it right every time (i.e., only blocked fraudulent charges) [189]. However, 37% of the people said *every* blocked charge was a legitimate purchase, i.e., false alarm. Another 15% said *most* of the blocked charges were legitimate.

Anomaly detection for cyber security, however, is a much broader and more challenging problem than the fraud detection in the payment industry. Some applications share similarities with the fraud detection, e.g., compromised accounts detection at social networking services. Some are quite different, e.g., the discovery of Indicators of Compromise (IOC) in cyber threat hunting.

As shown in previous chapters, the complexity of anomaly detection for general cyber security comes from the immense space of normal behaviors at all levels, including network traffic (network anomaly detection), inter-process communication (host anomaly detection), intra-process operation (program anomaly detection), and event-driven system activities (user behavior anomaly detection). Modern attacks usually exploit multiple aspects of a system, such as software vulnerabilities, phishing, policy enforcement errors, and unmanaged information channels.

Incomplete modeling raises isolated and partial alerts, which may be inadequate for defending against modern advanced persistent threats (APTs). Isolated anomaly detection techniques may yield high volumes of noise (false positives) in order to maintain high detection rates. A more promising threat intelligence system depends on monitoring systems across different levels, integrating observations to eliminate false positives, and efficiently involving human analysts.

8.2   SECURITY OPERATION CENTERS (SOC)

Cyber security is a complicated task for organizations of any size. On average, an organization generates over 200,000 security events per day; less than 100 are confirmed as attacks; 2 significant threats are identified per week on average [233]. It is common that an enterprise runs dozens of security products to cover the protection of endpoints, networks, sensitive data, access control, information services, etc. In case of security incidents, service/data recovery and incident inspection are needed for mitigating the damage and preventing further loss. Maintaining organizational security requires an investment in the infrastructure, software, utilities, and human capital.

Security Operation Centers (SOC) are created for collecting security events, performing attack/threat detection, sharing threat intelligence, and coordinating incident responses. Typically, SOC integrates a collection of security software from various vendors, triages and investigates hundreds of thousands of events per day, and leverages human intelligence in the operations. Examples of such SOCs include the U.S. Department of Homeland Security (DHS)'s National Cybersecurity and Communications Integration Center (NCCIC) [199] and Visa's Cyber Fusion Center [225].

A Security Operation Center is a department or division in an organization which processes organization-wide security events, discovers and evaluates threats, and responds to incidents for maintaining confidentiality, integrity, and availability of the organization's systems and data. It is the hub for security information exchange and command and control center, especially in the time of intrusion outbreaks.

Other than receiving millions of security-related records and processing them, modern SOC analysts are typically supported by Security Information and Event Management (SIEM) systems. SIEM is a tool to manage incoming events as well as security knowledge, classify the information, triage messages, infer correlations, visualize intermediate results, and integrate automatic detection. SIEM consumes logs from either running systems, e.g., web servers, workstations, and DNS servers, or security systems, e.g., endpoint detection systems, network firewalls, and intrusion detection systems (IDS). The advantage of the SIEM system is that it frees SOC analysts from mundane and repetitive tasks, such as mapping IP addresses in network firewall logs to domain name queries on organization DNS.

Compared to the huge volume of information collected, the amount of real attacks and threats is relatively small. Thus, the cyber defense procedure in enterprises is a pyramid structure, which is shown in Figure 8.1. This pyramid describes the procedure for distilling threat intelligence. Cyber-related information moves from the bottom of the pyramid to the top, from raw logs to security insights and knowledge.

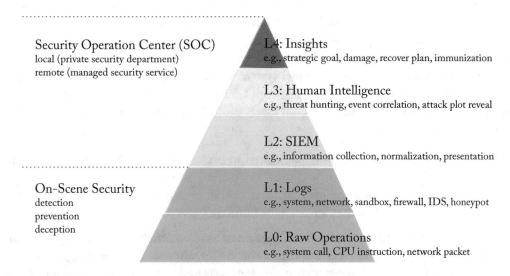

Figure 8.1: Enterprise cyber security pyramid.

The bottom half of the enterprise cyber security pyramid (on-scene security) is built into the organizational information infrastructure and operated distributedly. It records security information and provides local or/and real-time responses to events. L0 (Layer 0) denotes the information in the infrastructure of the organization, and L1 (Layer 1) provides basic security analysis and performs some real-time responses to malicious events, such as access control and intrusion prevention. The responses are primarily based on the *local* view of attacks, mostly Indicators of Compromise (IOCs), so that different response systems are autonomous, having little dependency on each other and have fast decision and response cycles.

Moving from the bottom half to the top half (security operation center) of the pyramid changes the data processing model from a distributed procedure to a centralized method. The aim is to discover connections between IOCs, find missing or hidden components, and provide an organizational vision for attack discovery. The top half pyramid can either be operated locally at the organization or remotely by a named managed security service provider (MSSP), e.g., Alienvault, IBM, or Trustwave.

While the enterprise cyber security pyramid provides a layered abstraction of information distillation and threat intelligence in organizations, real-world implementations may have cross-layer information flow. For instance, vertical channels can be created on L2 for human analysts to consume IDS reports directly and get insights into an attack.

8.3   ANOMALY DETECTION IN THE PYRAMID

Each layer of the pyramid above consists of distinct programmed or analytical methods for information distillation. Every method takes the advantage of either (i) the knowledge of known malicious activities or (ii) the knowledge of known benign/normal activities. Two classic examples of the former are signature-based anti-virus scanners and rule-based firewalls, while an example of the latter is anomaly detection.

Anomaly detection leverages normal system activities to detect aberrant and suspicious activities. Typically, all intermediate layers (from L1 to L3) of the security pyramid can involve some forms of anomaly detection. At each layer, anomaly detection consumes different input and has different detection goals.

- **L1**: anomaly detection can be implemented to perform local analysis during or after log extraction. System monitoring and simple detection take place in a distributed fashion at this layer. Anomaly detection approaches in this layer usually focus on one particular data type, e.g., system call, network packet, or CPU usage.

  Table 8.1 gives some examples of L1 products with anomaly detection functionalities. Avast antivirus software creates a sandbox at each endpoint. Unknown or suspicious binaries are executed and inspected in the sandbox, before requesting for comprehensive analysis. Various program anomaly detection methods are implemented in the sandbox to evaluate how suspicious the program is regarding its runtime behavior, e.g., system calls, file access patterns, network connections. Some L1 products focus on anomalous network traffic or packets detection, e.g., Statistical Packet Anomaly Detection Engine (SPADE) is a Snort [229] pre-processor plug-in that keeps track of different types of packets and reports abnormal packet distributions [23]. Other products such as *Application Manager* from ManageEngine work only on time series, e.g., CPU usage, the number of processed requests.

Table 8.1: Anomaly detection in L1 products

Vendor	L1 Product	Anomaly
Avast	Antivirus	Program behavior
Fortinet	Intrusion prevention system	Protocol
LogRhythm	User and entity behavior analytics	Endpoint
ManageEngine	Applications manager	Performance
RSA	Siver Tail	Network
Silicon Defence	Statistical packet anomaly detection engine	network packet
SolarWinds	Snort IDS log analysis	network

- **L2**: Behavior analysis is a key component in SIEM systems. SIEM consumes a large amount of data from distributedly operated L1 systems, connects the activity fragments, infers behaviors from the flows. It also classifies behaviors for attack discovery. Anomaly detection in SIEM can help discover uncommon or unknown behaviors for further inspection.

  Table 8.2 lists popular SIEM systems and their anomaly detection functionality. Some of them extend time-series anomaly detection mechanisms from L1 systems to L2 systems. The major difference between L1 and L2 time-series anomaly detection is the scope of operation. L2 algorithms describe normal and anomalous time-series in a large space since different user and system behaviors from multiple L1 feeding points are aggregated. However, the larger space usually results in a noisier series, which makes it more challenging to perform detection.

  Some SIEM systems bring their L2 anomaly detection tightly coupled with L2 specific information, such as user and system behaviors inferred from a set of connected L1 systems. For instance, LogRhythm system identifies users and entities from related L1 streams. The system builds user models and checks incoming user behavior regarding the models for detecting compromised accounts, privilege abuse, brute force, data exfiltration, etc.

- **L3**: Existing automatic detection systems are far from perfect in terms of their semantic awareness, self-learning capability, and detection accuracy. It is inevitable that human analysts have to be involved in the detection procedure.

  Human intelligence complements the incomplete domain knowledge encoded in detection programs. For example, by looking at a dense sequence of file access system calls to /proc/ in Linux or Android systems, human analysts can infer a process scanning behavior, which may not have been implemented as a signature in existing detection strategies.

Table 8.2: Anomaly detection capability of L2 SIEM systems

Vendor	L2 SIEM Product	Anomaly Detection Emphasis
EventTracker	Security center	General behavior analysis
HPE	ArchSight	Peer group analysis
IBM	QRadar	Traffic behavior analysis
LogRhythm	LogRythm	User and entity analysis
Micro Focus	Sentinel Enterprise	Environment analysis
Splunk	Enterprise security	Statistical and behavioral analysis
Trustwave	SIEM Enterprise	Network behavior analysis

Anomaly detection requires accessing and linking domain knowledge on the fly. Human analysts can help with (i) discovering anomalous patterns and (ii) ruling out false positives. For instance, an `Nginx` process initializes a connection to another machine inside the company. A human analyst with web server experiences would be more likely to point out this log entry as an anomaly than network anomaly detection, especially if the server has other processes frequently initializing network connections. Anomalies do not always indicate attacks or threats. Human analysts may help eliminate false alarms due to system upgrades, service adjustments, or seasonal patterns.

IBM's *Watson for Cyber* is an attempt toward assisting human analysts with digesting massive amounts of news articles and security literature. We describe it in Section 8.5. The related topic of building a knowledge base for anomaly detection is discussed in Chapter 9.

8.4 BUILDING YOUR OWN ANOMALY DETECTION TOOLKIT

This section discusses some of the free or open source tools for hosting anomaly or intrusion detection. In addition, generic machine-learning tools, such as *Weka* [254], ELKI [7], *scikit-learn* [212], and *TensorFlow* [4] are useful.

- *Apache Spot* [11] is an open source anomaly detection platform for network intrusion detection. It processes NetFlow, DNS, and proxy data through Spark and HDFS. And it leverages machine learning, e.g., topic modeling, to profile normal network activities and DNS packet payloads. Basic data processing and information distillation techniques are implemented, including Latent Dirichlet Allocation (LDA). Some analytics components are provided with Spot GUI, a visualization tool for human inspection and interaction.

- *Open Source Tripwire* [140] is a data integrity tool that generates alerts on specific file changes. It is originally developed and open sourced by Tripwire Inc. Tripwire is simple but good for learning basic concepts of anomaly detection in the field of cyber security: defining *self* and detecting *non-self*. With proper definitions of self or normal states, tripwire detects anomalies such as unauthorized file creation in /opt/nginx.

- *OSSEC* (Open Source HIDS SECurity) [121] is an open source Host-based Intrusion Detection System (HIDS) that provides basic host monitoring on varieties of operating systems from FreeBSD to Windows. It is supported by Alienvault and included in Alienvault Unified Security Management (USM) platform. OSSEC includes two major detection programs, Syscheck and Rootcheck, along with other scripts for detection and reaction. Rootcheck leverages anomaly detection as one of the mechanisms to perform rootkit detection.

- *OSSIM* (Open Source Security Information Management) [123] is an open source SIEM platform developed and released by Alienvault. It retrieves logs from mainstream server programs, e.g., IIS, operating systems, e.g., UNIX syslog, and IDS systems, e.g., Snort, for aggregation and further analysis.

  OSSIM includes a collection of L1 (Layer 1) software that performs anomaly detection: Spade identifies unusual connections based on packet header information; P0f detects operating system changes; Passive Real-time Asset Detection system (PRADS) [86] discovers network service changes. More advanced L2 and L3 anomaly detection mechanisms are open for development.

- *Apache Metron* [10] is a big data processing framework designed to ingest, process, and store diverse security feeds in the next-generation SOC. It evolves from Cisco OpenSOC with big data support from Storm, Kafka, HBase, etc. Currently, it supports data feeds from Snort, Bro, and NetFlow. More commercial feeds such as FireEye, Palo Alto Network, and CarbonBlack, are to be added. Metro provides a scalable framework for developing, testing, and deploying anomaly detection algorithms.

- *Security Onion* [234] is an Ubuntu-based Linux distribution that comes with a series of tools for deploying sensors, harvesting logs, and performing analysis such as anomaly detection. The distribution is supported by *Security Onion Solutions, LLC*, which provides training and operating services to its customers.

  Security Onion consists of three main components besides generic Linux kernel and utilities: (i) traffic dump, i.e., netsniff-ng, (ii) host- and network-based intrusion detection systems (HIDS and NIDS) such as Snort, Bro [210], Suricata [93] and OSSEC, and (iii) analysis toolkits including Sguil [287], Squert [118], Enterprise Log Search, and Archive (ELSA) [127].

Security Onion provides an example of constructing the cyber detection pipeline from the data sources (sensor deployment) to data sinks (log processing and analytic programs). Users can run anomaly detection scripts shipped with the distribution [60, 93, 280] or develop their algorithms to take advantage of the out-of-box monitoring and data collection capability.

- *Splunk* [139] is a data analysis tool that applies to security data with or without security semantics. It is developed by Splunk Inc. The free version of Splunk Lite focuses on generic machine learning and data analytics. The free version of Splunk User Behavior Analytics (Splunk UBA) is a piece of L2 software that works with SIEM systems. It is built upon Hadoop and relies on machine learning algorithms for computing risk scores and identifying anomalies.

- *Anomaly Detection* [151] is a statistically robust time-series anomaly detection R package. Twitter Inc. led its early development and released it in 2015. The package is not specifically designed for security, but supports a wide range of security detection applications on time-series data, e.g., CPU usage, network traffic processing speed. The highlight of the package is the algorithm named Seasonal Hybrid ESD (S-H-ESD), which performs time-series decomposition and supports both global and local anomaly detection.

- *EGADS* (Extensible Generic Anomaly Detection System) [162] is an open-source Java package that provides anomaly detection on large scale time-series datasets. It is a generic time-series anomaly detection library similar to the Twitter R package. It can be used in the context of cyber security, but the data is limited to time-series. One of the highlights is the capability to extract seasonal, trend, and noise patterns.

- *Surus* [137] is a collection of user defined functions (UDF) for Pig and Hive scripts that implement Robust Anomaly Detection (RAD) [138] and other functionalities. It is released by Netflix and focuses on big data analytics with Hadoop and Hive. RAD leverages robust Principal Component Analysis (rPCA) for anomaly detection, which can handle seasonal and irregularly distributed time-series.

8.5 LEVERAGING EXTERNAL KNOWLEDGE IN CYBER SECURITY PYRAMID

Being well informed is important to achieving enterprise security. In this section, we discuss how enterprises and organizations keep each other informed and explain the external information sources of the security pyramid. Knowledge sharing at the enterprise level happens through three main channels, which are explained next. Figure 8.2 illustrates these enterprise knowledge sharing channels.

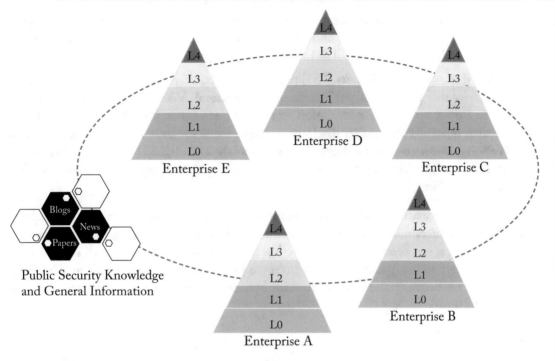

Figure 8.2: Enterprise security knowledge sharing around the globe.

- *Security service feedback*: Cyber security firms collect information from their customers about attack indicators or matched signatures. The information is processed into knowledge and redistributed to other parties for protection around the globe. The procedure usually happens at L1. Anti-virus signatures on endpoint protection systems is an example. They are distilled from reported malware samples and distributed to all endpoint detection systems across companies and organizations.

- *Information sharing alliance*: Some organizations have agreements with each other to share cyber intelligence information. Some security service providers play as a hub in the alliance for defining the interface and providing the infrastructure for information or knowledge sharing. X-Force Exchange owned by IBM is an example of the intelligence information sharing platform. Companies or organizations contribute and consume information regarding attacks and threats. SOC analysts at the L3 layer benefit from the information of other pyramids.

- *Public information retrieval*: When Wannacry broke out in 2017, security blogs and forums became the front line for sharing prevention and recovery solutions. It is vital for security analysts to be aware of the publicly available knowledge. Unfortunately, the sheer volume of the ever-growing information is intimidating. No human analysts could read 180 K pieces of security news articles and 720 K blog posts every year [92], let alone billions of records of blacklisted binaries, URLs, and IP addresses (e.g., on VirusTotal).

IBM's *Watson for Cyber Security* [135] project and *QRadar Advisor with Watson* system aim to address this problem of public information retrieval. Watson for Cyber Security can digest a huge amount of information from public resources, including threat databases, research reports, vulnerability disclosures, blogs, social media, etc. QRadar Advisor with Watson expresses the distilled knowledge with analytics in IBM QRadar SIEM system. It provides analysts with additional information along with analysis results to improve their decision making.

Existing information sharing infrastructures in the industry are for distributing malware signatures and vulnerabilities. Sharing for anomaly detection leveraging the same infrastructures, however, has not been reported. In Section 6.2.3, we describe the research effort on collaborative content anomaly detection in AutoSense [25], and explain the challenges involved. In Chapter 9, we further point out the need for building a comprehensive knowledge base for anomaly detection.

SUMMARY

Recent years have witnessed a massive growth of interests in anomaly detection algorithms and applications in a wide range of industries. In this chapter, we gave an overview of anomaly detection in the security industry and described anomaly detection components in commercial products at various levels. Despite its increasing popularity and some isolated successes, anomaly detection is still at its experimental stage in the industry. While virtually every security firm has anomaly detection built into their product lines, a mature anomaly detection system that can either (i) be deployed in a scalable manner with reliable detection or (ii) be operated as a service has not been reported.

CHAPTER 9

Exciting New Problems and Opportunities

In the previous chapters, we have described the technical challenges and state-of-the-art solutions for anomaly detection. We have covered various key aspects, including the evolution of anomaly detection, its fundamental limitations, new data-oriented threats, the challenge of diverse program behaviors, the role of program analysis in data science, requirements posed by cyber-physical environments, sensemaking of network traffic, adaptive and automatic anomaly detection, and the industry's perspective.

This is an exciting time to work on data-driven anomaly detection. The community is on the cusp of observing major breakthroughs. We close the book by highlighting some of the exciting new problems and opportunities, including order-aware recognition, instruction-level detection, automated deployment, and post-detection program repair. In addition, throughout the summaries of previous chapters, we have been pointing out new opportunities associated with outsourcing anomaly detection to service providers and lifting the operations to the cloud.

9.1 DEEP LEARNING AND INSTRUCTION-LEVEL ANOMALY DETECTION

How feasible is deep learning at solving tough anomaly detection problems, such as order-aware recognition and instruction-level anomaly detection?

We explain the problem of order-aware recognition. Consider an ordered sequence abcba. The set of adjacent call-pairs (2-tuples) in that sequence is {ab, bc, cb, ba}. Consider the other two different ordered sequences, cbabc and bcbab. Their sets of 2-tuples are identical to abcba's, as shown in Table 9.1. In comparison, their 3-tuple sets of these sequences are different.

Unfortunately, virtually all existing local and global anomaly detection are limited in discerning the order of long sequences. Many solutions are based on 2-dimensional matrices, i.e., call pairs or 2-tuples. For example, STILO [304] and STILO-context [302] used the first-order HMM, which is stateless and only captures pairwise patterns. HMMs do maintain probability values for call pairs, which may provide additional information for resolving collisions depicted in Table 9.1. However, higher-order pattern information is not captured by the models.[1] Using a large n in n-gram based detection would help. However, besides the significantly increased complexity, a large n does not fundamentally solve the problem, as collisions at the level of n-grams may still occur.

Table 9.1: An example illustrating the importance of recognizing the order in call sequences. The 2-tuple sets are identical for the three different sequences, i.e., collisions, whereas their 3-tuple sets are different.

Sequence	2-tuple	3-tuple
abcba	{ab, bc, cb, ba}	{abc, bcb, cba}
cbabc	{cb, ba, ab, bc}	{cba, bab, abc}
bcbab	{bc, cb, ba, ab}	{bcb, cba, bab}

We coined the phrase *deep anomaly detection* to refer to the use of deep learning in anomaly detection. Deep learning algorithms, such as Long Short-Term Memory (LSTM), together with the distributed TensorFlow framework,[2] may be promising in solving the above problem. LSTM is the state-of-the-art instantiation of the Recurrent Neural Network (RNN) approach. RNN does not make the Markov assumption (i.e., the present state alone determines the conditional probability distribution of future states) as HMM does. RNN takes into account longer dependencies. Therefore, RNN would be much better suited than HMM to answer the binary classification problem of *Given a call sequence $c_1, \ldots, c_k$, whether or not the sequence should occur?*

However, because our inputs (call/statement/instruction sequences) are semantically different from the inputs in typical deep learning applications (e.g., review sentiment recognition, handwriting recognition), existing RNN-based binary classification cannot be directly used. In addition, it is unclear how well LSTM handles extremely long inputs, as the current demonstrations have been on sentences in natural languages. Some studies on LSTM for security exist [83, 154], however, more thorough experimental demonstration is needed.

Another exciting research direction is instruction-level anomaly detection. Tracing instructions[3] is now made efficient by Intel PT, however, instruction-level anomaly detection has not been demonstrated in the literature. Virtually all existing detection is performed at a higher level, e.g., system-call, library-call, or function-call level. Data at the higher level has more semantics about the program, which is helpful in terms of designing algorithms, analyzing results, and utilizing tools. However, if an attack does not issue any systems/library/function calls, then it can completely bypass the detection. The return-oriented programming (ROP) and data-oriented programming (DOP) both have such a capability. Instruction-level detec-

---

[1] Some special sequences do not have information loss after the matrix conversion, e.g., a sequence consisting of all distinct calls.
[2] https://www.tensorflow.org/
[3] Only executions that impact the control flow are recorded by PT.

tion will potentially stop these exploits. However, the problem seems tough. For example, when executing a simple `ls` command, PT records a whopping 85,204 long addresses (e.g., `block: 7f3d2706bdc7` from dependent libraries) and 110 short addresses (e.g., `block: 40e9ec` from the application). These are just from tracing the user-level execution, excluding the kernel-level execution. With the massive amount of low-level entries, finding an anomaly is similar to finding a needle in a haystack. Demonstrating instruction-level anomaly detection is a worthy endeavor.

9.2   POST-DETECTION FORENSIC, REPAIR, AND RECOVERY

What should people do after they detect anomalies?

Cybersecurity research has been focusing on automatic detection, prevention, as well as proof-of-concept attack development. A huge missing link in the cybersecurity ecosystem is the lack of systematic research on security recovery, specifically on automatic vulnerability localization and program repair. As explained in Chapter 2, attributing the detected anomalies to a specific threat is challenging. Current common practices rely on manual effort. Upon anomaly alerts, security analysts would need to first localize and pinpoint the problematic code region. This localization process to identify root causes in code may be extremely challenging. Then, the developers need to manually generate patches for code repair through code insertion, deletion, or modification.

Substantial advances have been reported in the programming language and software engineering literature on automatic bug repair. Notable work includes genetic programming [113], templates mined from human patches [153], and machine learning of successful patches [177]. Virtually all of these techniques (and corresponding evaluation) are designed to find inadvertent programming errors. For example, most of the defects in existing defect benchmarks `ManyBugs` and `IntroClass` [114] do not impact security. In the `ManyBugs` benchmark, more than half of the instances impact correctness, not necessary security. It remains an open problem as to demonstrate a secure software ecosystem that enables the automatic or semi-automatic anomaly detection, localization of root causes of anomalies, and repair of vulnerable code, including those that may lead to stealthy exploits. A related interesting question includes *Is it possible to completely take the human out of the loop for security tasks?*

9.3   ANOMALY DETECTION OF CONCURRENCY ATTACKS

What does it take to detect anomalies in concurrent execution?

Yang et al. demonstrated that concurrency attacks are indeed possible [307]. Their work showed multiple exploitable concurrency errors, besides the familiar file system Time-of-Check-to-Time-of-Use (TOCTOU) races. For example, Figure 9.1 gives a concurrency error that corrupts the user identities, and allows privilege escalation attacks [307]. This bug is caused by Glibc's default thread library, `nptl`, not handling `setuid()` atomically. Function `__nptl_setxid()` in Figure 9.1 iterates through a list of all threads and signals each thread to call `setuid()` (line 6–12). However, this function releases the lock `stack_cache_lock` protecting the thread list, before it waits for all threads to finish setting their identifiers. A new thread may be created, and still have the old user identifiers. Because `setuid()` is often called to drop privileges, a thread skipping `setuid()` can thus result in privilege escalation.

```
 1 : __nptl_setxid (struct xid_command *cmdp)
 2 : {
 3 :    lll_lock (stack_cache_lock);
 4 :    // signal all threads on list to set user id.
 5 :    // a thread is represented as a stack
 6 :    list_for_each (runp, &stack_used)
 7 :    {
 8 :        struct pthread *t = list_entry (runp, struct pthread, list);
 9 :        if (t == self)
10:            continue;
11:        setxid_signal_thread (cmdp, t);
12:    }
13:    lll_unlock (stack_cache_lock);
14:    // ERROR: does not wait for other threads to acknowledge
15: }
16: allocate_stack(...) { // called when a new thread is created
17:    lll_lock (stack_cache_lock);
18:    list_add (&pd->list, &stack_used);
19:    lll_unlock (stack_cache _lock);
20: }
```

Figure 9.1: Glibc setuid race [307].

The authors observed that ability to exploit a concurrency error depends on the size of the timing window within which the error may occur. An attacker can expand this window through carefully crafted inputs. Their study also shows that many common mechanisms (e.g., taint tracking) in existing defenses would not work against concurrency attacks. The authors published their raw data including URLs to the concurrency errors and some exploits [306].

Detecting concurrency anomalies presents challenges. Intuitively, if an anomaly detector learns behaviors only with respect to a single thread in a multithreaded system, it may miss anomalies involving multiple threads. On the flip side, if the anomaly detector models behaviors of all threads, the model may become overly complex and noisy [307]. Anomaly detection of time series [245] might be relevant to this problem. However, the granularity of time required by concurrency-attack detection (e.g., ns for memory race and ms for file-system race) is much smaller than that of typical time-series anomaly-detection work [151] (e.g., days or months).

In addition, tracing at a much finer granularity (e.g., memory level) will be necessary, which will be expensive. In that regard, a related recent development is MPI, which is a new technique for recording program execution for auditing and forensic purposes [181]. MPI's key feature is the ability to partition execution based on the application-specific task structures. As part of this execution partition effort, MPI provides threading support for the browser. Specifically it recognizes the logical dependencies among interleaved threads.

9.4 MIMICRY GENERATION, INSIDER THREAT DETECTION, AUTOMATION, AND KNOWLEDGE BASE

To add to the previous list of open questions, in this section we point out a few more unsolved challenges associated with (i) generation of mimicry attacks, (ii) organization-wide anomaly detection, and (iii) automation of deployment and maintenance. This list is by no means complete.

- **Automatic Generation of Mimicry Attack Sequences**

  Given an anomaly detection algorithm and an attack goal, how to automatically construct an attack sequence that accomplishes the attack while evading the detection?

  Understanding adversaries' capabilities and limitations is an important part of building defenses. Researchers demonstrated the evasion of supervised PDF-malware-detection classifiers, such as PDFRATE [22, 288, 305]. PDFRATE is an online service for detection of PDF malware. It employs Random Forest algorithms to classify PDF files into benign or malicious. The classification is based on metadata and structural features of PDFs [288]. Evasion attacks modify the submitted PDF file, so that its malicious functionality remains intact, while the malware score returned by PDFRATE is decreased. For example, the evasion technique presented by Šrndić and Laskov is based on inserting dummy content into PDF files. The dummy content is ignored by PDF renderers, however, it affects the computation of features used in PDFRATE [288]. PDF malware can be generated automatically. However, for mimicry attacks (described in Chapter 2) against machine-learning based anomaly detection (e.g., HMM or SVM), it remains an open question as to what it takes to efficiently automate the generation of attack traces for arbitrary attack goals.

- **Insider Threat Detection**

  Will insider threat detection raise excessive numbers of false alarms in practice?

  Because of the diversity (described in Chapter 3) and concept drift (described in Chapter 7) in normal behaviors, it may seem challenging (if feasible at all) to generalize anomaly detection to the scale of the entire organization for identifying malicious insiders. The only large-scale insider threat evaluation [237] found in the literature does not report or analyze false positives, as we have discussed in Section 2.3.

A relevant technique is information-flow tracking. For example, Panorama [311] offers host-wide, fine-grained, operating-system-aware, and dynamic taint tracking. The authors demonstrated its application in malicious information flow, specifically monitoring and investigating an unknown sample's information access and processing behavior to sensitive information. Panorama monitors each CPU instruction and DMA operation that manipulates tainted data in order to determine how the taint propagates.

Suppose in the near future there will be a generalized organization-wide information flow tracking mechanism and the tracking can reach across service and machine boundaries. However, such a solution alone cannot stop insider threats. Tracking is only half of the solution. The other half is to determine whether the observed information-flow patterns are normal. Because malicious insiders have the access permissions, their activities would not trigger information-flow violations. In order to reveal abusive and abnormal data-access patterns, one needs to analyze information flows *quantitatively*, e.g., frequencies, correlations, co-occurrences, and conditional probabilities.

- **Encyclopedia of Anomaly Detection**

  The knowledge base will provide comprehensive guidance on all aspects of anomaly detection design and deployment.

  Such a moderated public platform will systematize the knowledge and resources from multiple communities, covering cyber security, data science, and various specific application domains (e.g., industry control, smart infrastructure, and healthcare). Some initial efforts toward systematizing the anomaly detection knowledge have already been reported. For example, Goldstein and Uchida gave a comparative evaluation of unsupervised anomaly detection algorithms (e.g., clustering, k-nearest neighbor, rPCA [37]) for multivariate data [111]. The work has interesting findings, e.g., the comparison evaluation suggested that nearest-neighbor based algorithms perform better in most cases when compared to clustering algorithms. Also, for example, when there is little knowledge about the nature of anomalies in the dataset, the authors recommended to first use a global anomaly detection algorithm [111]. With the rapid rise of data-driven inter-disciplinary anomaly detection needs, having a comprehensive knowledge base that provides fine-grained recommendations will be extremely beneficial to researchers and practitioners.

SUMMARY

In this chapter, we pointed out several new research and development opportunities. Exploring these exciting new directions will help realize the vision of democratizing anomaly detection technology, making it accessible to millions of people, including security analysts, domain experts, as well as non-tech-savvy individuals. This vision drives the design and development of low-maintenance products that security analysts can deploy in the real world, comprehensive tools that domain experts can use to solve their problems, and "smart" products that average users can use to protect their smart environments.

Bibliography

[1] Australian Defense Force Academy (ADFA) dataset. `https://research.unsw.edu.au/sites/all/files/facultyadmin/adfa-ids-database_license-homepage.pdf` 97

[2] Address Space Layout Randomization (ASLR), 2003. PaX Team. `http://pax.grsecurity.net/docs/aslr.txt` 5

[3] F. A. T. Abad, J. V. D. Woude, Y. Lu, S. Bak, M. Caccamo, L. Sha, R. Mancuso, and S. Mohan. On-chip control flow integrity check for real time embedded systems. In *IEEE 1st International Conference on Cyber-physical Systems, Networks, and Applications*, 2013. DOI: 10.1109/cpsna.2013.6614242. 53, 55

[4] Martín Abadi, Ashish Agarwal, Paul Barham, Eugene Brevdo, Zhifeng Chen, Craig Citro, Gregory S. Corrado, Andy Davis, Jeffrey Dean, Matthieu Devin, Sanjay Ghemawat, Ian J. Goodfellow, Andrew Harp, Geoffrey Irving, Michael Isard, Yangqing Jia, Rafal Józefowicz, Lukasz Kaiser, Manjunath Kudlur, Josh Levenberg, Dan Mané, Rajat Monga, Sherry Moore, Derek Gordon Murray, Chris Olah, Mike Schuster, Jonathon Shlens, Benoit Steiner, Ilya Sutskever, Kunal Talwar, Paul A. Tucker, Vincent Vanhoucke, Vijay Vasudevan, Fernanda B. Viégas, Oriol Vinyals, Pete Warden, Martin Wattenberg, Martin Wicke, Yuan Yu, and Xiaoqiang Zheng. TensorFlow: Large-scale machine learning on heterogeneous distributed systems. *CoRR*, abs/1603.04467, 2016. 104

[5] Martín Abadi, Mihai Budiu, Úlfar Erlingsson, and Jay Ligatti. Control-flow integrity: Principles, implementations, and applications. In *Proc. of the 12th ACM Conference on Computer and Communications Security, (CCS'05)*, pages 340–353, New York, 2005. DOI: 10.1145/1609956.1609960. 5, 8, 38, 53, 59, 62

[6] Tigist Abera, N. Asokan, Lucas Davi, Jan-Erik Ekberg, Thomas Nyman, Andrew Paverd, Ahmad-Reza Sadeghi, and Gene Tsudik. C-FLAT: Control-flow attestation for embedded systems software. In *Proc. of the ACM Conference on Computer and Communications Security (CCS)*, 2016. DOI: 10.1145/2976749.2978358. 53, 55, 57, 58, 59, 65, 66

[7] Elke Achtert, Hans-Peter Kriegel, and Arthur Zimek. ELKI: A software system for evaluation of subspace clustering algorithms. In *Proc. of the Scientific and Statistical Database Management, 20th International Conference, (SSDBM)*, pages 580–585, Hong Kong, China, July 9–11, 2008. DOI: 10.1007/978-3-540-69497-7_41. 104

[8] S. Adepu, S. Shrivastava, and A. Mathur. Argus: An orthogonal defense framework to protect public infrastructure against cyber-physical attacks. *IEEE Internet Computing*, 20(5):38–45, 2016. DOI: 10.1109/mic.2016.104. 58

[9] Aleph One. Smashing the stack for fun and profit, 1996. http://insecure.org/stf/smashstack.html 17

[10] Apache. Apache metron big data security. http://metron.apache.org/ 105

[11] Apache. Apache spot. http://spot.incubator.apache.org/ 104

[12] Arduino. www.arduino.cc/ 63

[13] ArduPilot Programming Libraries. ardupilot.org/dev/docs/ 60

[14] Daniel Arp, Michael Spreitzenbarth, Malte Hubner, Hugo Gascon, and Konrad Rieck. DREBIN: Effective and explainable detection of Android malware in your pocket. In *21st Annual Network and Distributed System Security Symposium, (NDSS)*, The Internet Society, San Diego, CA, February 23–26, 2014. DOI: 10.14722/ndss.2014.23247. 44

[15] George K. Baah, Andy Podgurski, and Mary Jean Harrold. The probabilistic program dependence graph and its application to fault diagnosis. In *Proc. of the International Symposium on Software Testing and Analysis, (ISSTA'08)*, pages 189–200, 2008. DOI: 10.1145/1390630.1390654. 42

[16] George K. Baah, Andy Podgurski, and Mary Jean Harrold. Causal inference for statistical fault localization. In *International Symposium on Software Testing and Analysis*, pages 73–84, 2010. DOI: 10.1145/1831708.1831717. 42

[17] P. V. Bahl, R. Chandra, A. Greenberg, S. Kandula, D. Maltz, and M. Zhang. Towards highly reliable enterprise network services via inference of multi-level dependencies. In *Proc. of ACM SIGCOMM*, August 2007. DOI: 10.1145/1282427.1282383. 69

[18] Lolita C. Baldor. Military: Computer virus wasn't directed at drones, 2011. http://www.nbcnews.com/id/44883383/ns/technology_and_science-security/t/military-computer-virus-wasnt-directed-drones/%23.W00401Pyub8 4, 5

[19] Alexandru G. Bardas, Sathya Chandran Sundaramurthy, Xinming Ou, and Scott A. De-Loach. MTD CBITS: Moving target defense for cloud-based IT systems. In *Proc. of the 22nd European Symposium on Research in Computer Security (ESORICS)*, Oslo, Norway, September 2017. DOI: 10.1007/978-3-319-66402-6_11. 5

[20] Asa Ben-Hur, David Horn, Hava T. Siegelmann, and Vladimir Vapnik. Support vector clustering. *Journal of Machine Learning Research*, 2:125–137, 2001. DOI: 10.4249/scholarpedia.5187. 23

[21] E. Bertino. Security threats: Protecting the new cyberfrontier. *Computer*, 49(6):11–14, 2016. DOI: 10.1109/mc.2016.188. 16

[22] Battista Biggio, Igino Corona, Davide Maiorca, Blaine Nelson, Nedim Šrndić, Pavel Laskov, Giorgio Giacinto, and Fabio Roli. Evasion attacks against machine learning at test time. In Hendrik Blockeel, Kristian Kersting, Siegfried Nijssen, and Filip Železný, Eds., *Machine Learning and Knowledge Discovery in Databases: European Conference, (ECML PKDD), Proceedings, Part III*, Prague, Czech Republic, September 23–27, 2013, Springer Berlin Heidelberg, pages 387–402, Berlin, Heidelberg, 2013. DOI: 10.1007/978-3-642-40994-3. 113

[23] Simon Biles. Detecting the unknown with Snort and the statistical packet anomaly detection engine (SPADE). http://pld.cs.luc.edu/courses/447/sum08/class6/biles.spade.pdf 102

[24] Andrea Bittau, Adam Belay, Ali José Mashtizadeh, David Mazières, and Dan Boneh. Hacking blind. In *IEEE Symposium on Security and Privacy, (SP)*, pages 227–242, Computer Society, Berkeley, CA, May 18–21, 2014. DOI: 10.1109/sp.2014.22. 5, 18

[25] Nathaniel Boggs, Sharath Hiremagalore, Angelos Stavrou, and Salvatore J. Stolfo. Cross-domain collaborative anomaly detection: So far yet so close. In Robin Sommer, Davide Balzarotti, and Gregor Maier, Eds., *Proc. of the Recent Advances in Intrusion Detection: 14th International Symposium, (RAID)*, Menlo Park, CA, September 20–21, 2011, pages 142–160, Springer Berlin Heidelberg, Berlin, Heidelberg, 2011. DOI: 10.1007/978-3-642-23644-0. 70, 71, 72, 108

[26] Brian M. Bowen, Pratap V. Prabhu, Vasileios P. Kemerlis, Stelios Sidiroglou, Angelos D. Keromytis, and Salvatore J. Stolfo. Botswindler: Tamper resistant injection of believable decoys in VM-based hosts for crimeware detection. In Somesh Jha, Robin Sommer, and Christian Kreibich, Eds., *Proc. of the Recent Advances in Intrusion Detection, 13th International Symposium, (RAID)*, Ottawa, Ontario, Canada, September 15–17, 2010, volume 6307 of *Lecture Notes in Computer Science*, pages 118–137, Springer, 2010. DOI: 10.1007/978-3-642-15512-3. 5

[27] Russell Brandom. UK hospitals hit with massive ransomware attack–sixteen hospitals shut down as a result of the attack, May 2017. https://www.theverge.com/2017/5/12/15630354/nhs-hospitals-ransomware-hack-wannacry-bitcoin 4

[28] Tevfik Bultan. Side channel analysis using a model counting constraint solver and symbolic execution. In *Proc. of the 5th ACM SIGPLAN International Workshop on the State Of the Art in Program Analysis (SOAP)*, Santa Barbara, CA, June 2016. 6

[29] Elie Bursztein. Why is applying machine learning to anti-abuse so hard? In *9th ACM Workshop on Artificial Intelligence and Security (AISec)*, Vienna, Austria, October 2016. Co-located with the ACM Conference on Computer and Communications (CCS). 1

[30] Patrick Butler, Kui Xu, and Danfeng Yao. Quantitatively analyzing stealthy communication channels. In *Proc. of the 9th International Conference on Applied Cryptography and Network Security (ACNS'11)*, number 6715 in Lecture Notes in Computer Science (LNCS), pages 238–254, 2011. DOI: 10.1007/978-3-642-21554-4_14. 22

[31] Nicholas Carlini, Antonio Barresi, Mathias Payer, David Wagner, and Thomas R. Gross. Control-flow bending: On the effectiveness of control-flow integrity. *24th USENIX Security Symposium (USENIX Security 15)*, pages 161–176, Washington, D.C., USENIX Association, 2015. https://www.usenix.org/conference/usenixsecurity15/techni cal-sessions/presentation/carlini 9

[32] Center for Applied Internet Data Analysis (CAIDA) dataset. http://www.caida.or g/data/overview/ 97

[33] Community Resource for Archiving Wireless Data At Dartmouth (CRAWDAD dataset). http://crawdad.org/ 97

[34] Call trace datasets for anomaly detection. http://people.cs.vt.edu/danfeng/sof tware.html#call-trace-dataset 96

[35] DAMI: Supplementary material for on the evaluation of unsupervised outlier detection: Measures, datasets, and an empirical study. http://lapad-web.icmc.usp.br/reposi tories/outlier-evaluation/DAMI/ 96

[36] Guilherme O. Campos, Arthur Zimek, Jörg Sander, Ricardo J. G. B. Campello, Barbora Micenková, Erich Schubert, Ira Assent, and Michael E. Houle. On the evaluation of unsupervised outlier detection: Measures, datasets, and an empirical study. *Data Mining and Knowledge Discovery*, 30(4):891–927, 2016. DOI: 10.1007/s10618-015-0444-8. 96

[37] Emmanuel J. Candès, Xiaodong Li, Yi Ma, and John Wright. Robust principal component analysis? *Journal of the Association for Computing Machinery*, 58(3):11:1–11:37, June 2011. DOI: 10.1145/1970392.1970395. 1, 2, 114

[38] Dawn M. Cappelli, Andrew P. Moore, and Randall F. Trzeciak. *The CERT Guide to Insider Threats: How to Prevent, Detect, and Respond to Information Technology Crimes (Theft, Sabotage, Fraud)*. Addison-Wesley Professional, 2012. 16, 97

[39] Alvaro A. Cárdenas, Saurabh Amin, Zong-Syun Lin, Yu-Lun Huang, Chi-Yen Huang, and Shankar Sastry. Attacks against process control systems: Risk assessment, detection, and response. In *Proc. of Association for Computing Machinery, (ASIACCS)*, 2011. DOI: 10.1145/1966913.1966959. 51, 54, 56

[40] Nicholas Carlini and David Wagner. ROP is still dangerous: Breaking modern defenses. In *Proc. of Usenix Security*, 2014. 5, 18

[41] Nicolas Carlini, Antonio Barresi, Mathias Payer, David Wagner, and Thomas R. Gross. Control-flow bending: On the effectiveness of control-flow integrity. In *USENIX Security*, 2015. 53

[42] M. Castro, M. Costa, and T. Harris. Securing software by enforcing data-flow integrity. In *Proc. of the 7th Symposium on Operating Systems Design and Implementation (OSDI)*, 2006. 5, 15

[43] Traffic causality dataset: HTTP requests and user events. `http://people.cs.vt.edu/danfeng/software.html#causality-dataset` 97

[44] Intel control-flow enforcement technology (CET) preview, 2016. 5, 9

[45] Lessons learned from Challenger, 1988. Safety division, NASA. `https://ocw.mit.edu/courses/aeronautics-and-astronautics/16-891j-space-policy-seminar-spring-2003/readings/challengerlessons.pdf` 13

[46] Varun Chandola, Arindam Banerjee, and Vipin Kumar. Anomaly detection: A survey. *ACM Computing Surveys*, 41(3):15:1–15:58, July 2009. DOI: 10.1145/1541880.1541882. 1, 3

[47] Stephen Checkoway, Damon McCoy, Brian Kantor, Danny Anderson, Hovav Shacham, Stefan Savage, Karl Koscher, Alexei Czeskis, Franziska Roesner, and Tadayoshi Kohno. Comprehensive experimental analyses of automotive attack surfaces. In *Proc. of the 20th USENIX Conference on Security (SEC'11)*, 2011. 52

[48] Daming D. Chen, Manuel Egele, Maverick Woo, and David Brumley. Towards automated dynamic analysis for Linux-based embedded firmware. In *Proc. of the Network and Distributed System Security Symposium (NDSS)*, 2016. DOI: 10.14722/ndss.2016.23415. 53

[49] Kai Chen, Peng Wang, Yeonjoon Lee, XiaoFeng Wang, Nan Zhang, Heqing Huang, Wei Zou, and Peng Liu. Finding unknown malice in 10 seconds: Mass vetting for new threats at the Google-play scale. In *Proc. of the 24th USENIX Conference on Security Symposium, (SEC'15)*, pages 659–674, USENIX Association, Berkeley, CA, 2015. 44

[50] Shuo Chen, Jun Xu, Emre C. Sezer, Prachi Gauriar, and Ravishankar K. Iyer. Non-control-data attacks are realistic threats. In *USENIX Security*, 2005. 8, 14, 15, 28

[51] X. Chen, M. Zhang, Z. M. Mao, and P. Bahl. Automating network application dependency discovery: Experiences, limitations, and new solutions. In *Proc. of OSDI*, pages 117–130, USENIX Association, 2008. 69

[52] Long Cheng, Fang Liu, and Danfeng Yao. Enterprise data breach: Causes, challenges, prevention, and future directions. *WIREs Data Mining and Knowledge Discovery*, 7, September/October 2017. DOI: 10.1002/widm.1211. 16, 17

[53] Long Cheng, Ke Tian, and Danfeng Yao. Enforcing cyber-physical execution semantics to defend against data-oriented attacks. In *Proc. of Annual Computer Security Applications Conference (ACSAC)*, Puerto Rico, December 2017. vi, 9, 27, 51, 54, 55, 56, 57, 58, 62, 63, 64, 65

[54] Erika Chin, Adrienne Porter Felt, Kate Greenwood, and David Wagner. Analyzing inter-application communication in Android. In *Proc. of the 9th International Conference on Mobile Systems, Applications, and Services, (MobiSys'11)*, pages 239–252, ACM, New York, 2011. DOI: 10.1145/1999995.2000018. 45

[55] Kyong-Tak Cho, Kang G. Shin, and Taejoon Park. CPS approach to checking norm operation of a brake-by-wire system. In *ICCPS*, 2015. DOI: 10.1145/2735960.2735977. 54, 56

[56] CIA to launch private app store. http://www.federaltimes.com/story/governmen t/it/cloud/2015/02/26/cia-private-app-store/24064285/ 45

[57] F. Cohen. Computer viruses: Theory and experiments. *Computer and Security*, 6(1):22–35, February 1987. DOI: 10.1016/0167-4048(87)90122-2. 3, 13, 18

[58] Robert Cohn. Part two: Optimizing Pintools. http://slideplayer.com/slide/ 9223282/ 92

[59] Eric Cole and Sandra Ring. *Insider Threat-protecting the Enterprise from Sabotage, Spying, and Theft*. Elsevier, 2006. 17

[60] Eric Conrad. C2 phone home: Leveraging SecurityOnion to identify command and control channels, September 2016. http://www.ericconrad.com/2016/09/c2-phon e-home-leveraging-securityonion.html 106

[61] Marco Cova, Davide Balzarotti, Viktoria Felmetsger, and Giovanni Vigna. Swaddler: An approach for the anomaly-based detection of state violations in web applications. In *Proc. of the International Symposium on Research in Attacks, Intrusions and Defenses*, pages 63–86, 2007. DOI: 10.1007/978-3-540-74320-0_4. 6, 15, 28

[62] Benjamin Cox, David Evans, Adrian Filipi, Jonathan Rowanhill, Wei Hu, Jack Davidson, John Knight, Anh Nguyen-tuong, and Jason Hiser. N-variant systems: A secretless framework for security through diversity. In *Proc. of the 15th USENIX Security Symposium*, pages 105–120, 2006. 5

[63] Tanya L. Crenshaw, Elsa L. Gunter, Craig L. Robinson, Lui Sha, and P. R. Kumar. The simplex reference model: Limiting fault-propagation due to unreliable components in cyber-physical system architectures. In *Proc. of the 28th IEEE Real-time Systems Symposium (RTSS)*, pages 400–412, Tucson, Arizona, December 3–6, 2007. DOI: 10.1109/rtss.2007.34. 14

[64] Gabriela F. Cretu, Angelos Stavrou, Michael E. Locasto, Salvatore J. Stolfo, and Angelos D. Keromytis. Casting out demons: Sanitizing training data for anomaly sensors. In *Proc. of IEEE Symposium on Security and Privacy (SP'08)*, pages 81–95, 2008. DOI: 10.1109/sp.2008.11. 8, 21, 79, 81, 82, 83, 84, 85

[65] Gabriela F. Cretu-Ciocarlie. *Towards self-adaptive anomaly detection sensors*. Ph.D. thesis, Columbia University, 2009. vi

[66] Gabriela F. Cretu-Ciocarlie, Angelos Stavrou, Michael E. Locasto, and Salvatore J. Stolfo. Adaptive anomaly detection via self-calibration and dynamic updating. In Engin Kirda, Somesh Jha, and Davide Balzarotti, Eds., *Proc. of the Recent Advances in Intrusion Detection: 12th International Symposium, (RAID)*, Saint-Malo, France, September 23–25, pages 41–60, Springer Berlin Heidelberg, Berlin, Heidelberg, 2009. 8, 79, 80, 85, 86, 87, 88, 89, 90, 91

[67] Bo Cui, Y. Zhu, H. Guan, and B. Yang. Anomaly forecast—useful tool for extreme weather detection. In *94th American Meteorological Society Annual Meeting*, 2014. 1

[68] Weidong Cui, Randy H. Katz, and Wai-tian Tan. BINDER: An extrusion-based break-in detector for personal computers. Technical Report UCB/CSD-04-1352, EECS Department, University of California, Berkeley, October 2004. 68

[69] Weidong Cui, Y H. Katz, and Wai tian Tan. BINDER: An extrusion-based break-in detector for personal computers. In *Proc. USENIX Annual Technical Conference*, page 4, 2005. 67, 68

[70] Marc Damashek. Gauging similarity with n-grams: Language-independent categorization of text. *Science*, 267(5199):843–848, February 1995. DOI: 10.1126/science.267.5199.843. 25

[71] Mahashweta Das and Srinivasan Parthasarathy. Anomaly detection and spatio-temporal analysis of global climate system. In *Proc. of the 3rd International Workshop on Knowledge Discovery from Sensor Data, (SensorKDD'09)*, pages 142–150, ACM, New York, 2009. DOI: 10.1145/1601966.1601989. 1

[72] Dorothy E. Denning. An intrusion-detection model. *IEEE Transactions Software Engineering*, 13(2):222–232, February 1987. DOI: 10.1109/tse.1987.232894. 1, 2, 6, 7

[73] Patricia Derler, Edward A. Lee, Stavros Tripakis, and Martin Törngren. Cyber-physical system design contracts. In *ICCPS*, 2013. DOI: 10.1145/2502524.2502540. 51

[74] Andreas Dewald, Thorsten Holz, and Felix C. Freiling. ADSandbox: Sandboxing Javascript to fight malicious websites. In *Proc. of the Symposium on Applied Computing, (SAC'10)*, pages 1859–1864, ACM, New York, 2010. DOI: 10.1145/1774088.1774482. 24

[75] Defense information systems agency: The IT combat support agency. http://www.disa.mil/cybersecurity 5

[76] Double Helix: High assurance N-variant systems. http://www.jackwdavidson.com/page/page-4/ 5

[77] Karim O. Elish. *User-Intention Based Program Analysis for Android Security*. Ph.D. thesis, Virginia Tech, 2015. vi

[78] Karim O. Elish, Xiaokui Shu, Danfeng (Daphne) Yao, Barbara G. Ryder, and Xuxian Jiang. Profiling user-trigger dependence for android malware detection. *Computers and Security*, 49:255–273, 2015. DOI: 10.1016/j.cose.2014.11.001. 44, 45, 46, 47, 48

[79] Charles Elkan. The foundations of cost-sensitive learning. In *International Joint Conference on Artificial Intelligence*, volume 17, pages 973–978, 2001. 76

[80] R. Elwell and R. Polikar. Incremental learning of concept drift in nonstationary environments. *IEEE Transactions on Neural Networks*, 22(10):1517–1531, October 2011. DOI: 10.1109/tnn.2011.2160459. 80

[81] Alex Endert, Patrick Fiaux, and Chris North. Semantic interaction for sensemaking: Inferring analytical reasoning for model steering. *IEEE Transactions on Visualization and Computer Graphics*, 18(12):2879–2888, 2012. DOI: 10.1109/tvcg.2012.260. 68

[82] Alex Endert, Patrick Fiaux, and Chris North. Semantic interaction for visual text analytics. In *Proc. of the SIGCHI Conference on Human Factors in Computing Systems, (CHI'12)*, pages 473–482, ACM, New York, 2012. DOI: 10.1145/2207676.2207741. 68

[83] Cheng Feng, Tingting Li, and Deeph Chana. Multi-level anomaly detection in industrial control systems via package signatures and LSTM networks. In *DSN*, 2017. DOI: 10.1109/dsn.2017.34. 53, 55, 110

[84] Henry Hanping Feng, Jonathon T. Giffin, Yong Huang, Somesh Jha, Wenke Lee, and Barton P. Miller. Formalizing sensitivity in static analysis for intrusion detection. In *Proc. of the IEEE Symposium on Security and Privacy*, pages 194–208, 2004. DOI: 10.1109/secpri.2004.1301324. 6, 8, 38, 66

[85] Henry Hanping Feng, Oleg M. Kolesnikov, Prahlad Fogla, Wenke Lee, and Weibo Gong. Anomaly detection using call stack information. In *Proc. of the IEEE Symposium on Security and Privacy*, pages 62–75, 2003. DOI: 10.1109/secpri.2003.1199328. 6

[86] Edward Fjellskål. Passive real-time asset detection system. `https://github.com/gamelinux/prads` 105

[87] Prahlad Fogla and Wenke Lee. Evading network anomaly detection systems: Formal reasoning and practical techniques. In *Proc. of the 13th Conference on Computer and Communications Security, (CCS'06)*, pages 59–68, ACM, New York, 2006. DOI: 10.1145/1180405.1180414. 19

[88] S. Forrest, S. A. Hofmeyr, and A. Somayaji. Intrusion detection using sequences of system calls. *Journal of Computer Security*, 6:151–180, 1998. DOI: 10.3233/jcs-980109. 6

[89] S. Forrest, A. Somayaji, and D. H. Ackley. Building diverse computer systems. In *Proc. of the 6th Workshop on Hot Topics in Operating Systems*, pages 67–72, May 1997. DOI: 10.1109/hotos.1997.595185. 5

[90] Stephanie Forrest, Steven Hofmeyr, and Anil Somayaji. The evolution of system-call monitoring. In *Proc. of the Annual Computer Security Applications Conference*, pages 418–430, 2008. DOI: 10.1109/acsac.2008.54. 6, 29

[91] Stephanie Forrest, Steven A. Hofmeyr, Anil Somayaji, and Thomas A. Longstaff. A sense of self for Unix processes. In *Proc. of the IEEE Symposium on Security and Privacy, (SP'96)*, IEEE Computer Society, Washington, DC, 1996. DOI: 10.1109/secpri.1996.502675. 6, 7, 25, 29

[92] Forrester. Can you give the business the data that it needs?, November 2013. 108

[93] Open information security foundation. Suricata. `https://suricata-ids.org/` 105, 106

[94] Aurélien Francillon and Claude Castelluccia. Code injection attacks on Harvard-architecture devices. In *CCS*, 2008. DOI: 10.1145/1455770.1455775. 53

[95] Aurélien Francillon, Daniele Perito, and Claude Castelluccia. Defending embedded systems against control flow attacks. In *SecuCode*, 2009. DOI: 10.1145/1655077.1655083. 53

[96] Alessandro Frossi, Federico Maggi, Gian Luigi Rizzo, and Stefano Zanero. Selecting and improving system call models for anomaly detection. In *Proc. of the 6th International Conference on Detection of Intrusions and malware, and Vulnerability Assessment, (DIMVA)*, 2009. DOI: 10.1007/978-3-642-02918-9_13. 29

[97] N. F. Galathy, B. Yuce, and P. Schaumont. A systematic approach to fault attack resistant design. In S. Bhunia, S. Ray, and S. Sur-Kolay, Eds., *Fundamentals of IP and SoC Security*, Springer, 2017. 14

[98] Debin Gao, Michael K. Reiter, and Dawn Song. On gray-box program tracking for anomaly detection. In *Proc. of USENIX Security*, volume 13, 2004. 18, 19, 20

[99] Debin Gao, Michael K. Reiter, and Dawn Song. Behavioral distance measurement using hidden Markov models. In *Proc. of the International Symposium on Research in Attacks, Intrusions and Defenses*, pages 19–40, 2006. DOI: 10.1007/11856214_2. 29

[100] Debin Gao, Michael K. Reiter, and Dawn Xiaodong Song. Beyond output voting: Detecting compromised replicas using HMM-based behavioral distance. *IEEE Transactions on Dependable and Secure Computing*, 6(2):96–110, 2009. DOI: 10.1109/tdsc.2008.39. 6, 26

[101] P. García-Teodoro, J. Díaz-Verdejo, G. Maciá-Fernández, and E. Vázquez. Anomaly-based network intrusion detection: Techniques, systems and challenges. *Computer Security*, 28(1-2):18–28, February 2009. DOI: 10.1016/j.cose.2008.08.003. 67

[102] Carrie Gates, Michael Franz, and John P. McDermott, Eds. *26th Annual Computer Security Applications Conference, (ACSAC)*, ACM, Austin, Texas, December 6–10, 2010. 137, 143

[103] Carrie Gates and Carol Taylor. Challenging the anomaly detection paradigm: A provocative discussion. In Christian Hempelmann and Victor Raskin, Eds., *Proc. of the New Security Paradigms Workshop*, Schloss Dagstuhl, Germany, September 19–22, ACM, pages 21–29, 2006. 81

[104] Xinyang Ge, Weidong Cui, and Trent Jaeger. GRIFFIN: Guarding control flows using Intel Processor Trace. In *Proc. of the 22nd International Conference on Architectural Support for Programming Languages and Operating Systems, (ASPLOS)*, pages 585–598, Xi'an, China, April 8–12, 2017. DOI: 10.1145/3037697.3037716. 10

[105] German steel mill meltdown. securityintelligence.com/german-steel-mill-meltdown-rising-stakes-in-the-internet-of-things/ 58

[106] Jonathon T. Giffin, David Dagon, Somesh Jha, Wenke Lee, and Barton P. Miller. Environment-sensitive intrusion detection. In *Proc. of the International Symposium on Research in Attacks, Intrusions and Defenses*, pages 185–206, 2006. DOI: 10.21236/ada448428. 6

[107] Jonathon T. Giffin, Somesh Jha, and Barton P. Miller. Efficient context-sensitive intrusion detection. In *Proc. of the Network and Distributed System Security Symposium (NDSS)*, 2004. 6, 8, 38

[108] Joshua Glasser and Brian Lindauer. Bridging the gap: A pragmatic approach to generating insider threat data. In *IEEE Symposium on Security and Privacy Workshops*, pages 98–104, IEEE Computer Society, Los Alamitos, CA, 2012. DOI: 10.1109/spw.2013.37. 97

[109] Enes Goktas, Elias Athanasopoulos, Herbert Bos, and Georgios Portokalidis. Out of control: Overcoming control-flow integrity. In *Proc. of the 35th IEEE Symposium on Security and Privacy*, San Jose, CA, May 2014. DOI: 10.1109/sp.2014.43. 5, 18

[110] Markus Goldstein and Seiichi Uchida. Unsupervised anomaly detection benchmark. https://dataverse.harvard.edu/dataset.xhtml?persistentId=doi:10.7910/DVN/OPQMVF 96

[111] Markus Goldstein and Seiichi Uchida. A comparative evaluation of unsupervised anomaly detection algorithms for multivariate data. *PLOS ONE*, 11(4):1–31, April 2016. DOI: 10.1371/journal.pone.0152173. 96, 114

[112] Rajeev Gopalakrishna, Eugene H. Spafford, and Jan Vitek. Efficient intrusion detection using automaton inlining. In *Proc. of the IEEE Symposium on Security and Privacy, (SP'05)*, pages 18–31, IEEE Computer Society, Washington, DC, 2005. DOI: 10.1109/sp.2005.1. 8, 38

[113] Claire Le Goues, Michael Dewey-Vogt, Stephanie Forrest, and Westley Weimer. A systematic study of automated program repair: Fixing 55 out of 105 bugs for $8 each. In *Proc. of International Conference on Software Engineering (ICSE)*, 2012. DOI: 10.1109/icse.2012.6227211. 111

[114] Claire Le Goues, Neal Holtschulte, Edward K. Smith, Yuriy Brun, Premkumar Devanbu, Stephanie Forrest, and Westley Weimer. The ManyBugs and IntroClass benchmarks for automated repair of C programs. *IEEE Transactions on Software Engineering*, 2015. DOI: 10.1109/tse.2015.2454513. 111

[115] T. M. Green, W. Ribarsky, and B. Fisher. Visual analytics for complex concepts using a human cognition model. In *IEEE Symposium on Visual Analytics Science and Technology*, pages 91–98, October 2008. DOI: 10.1109/vast.2008.4677361. 68

[116] J. Habibi, A. Gupta, S. Carlsony, A. Panicker, and E. Bertino. Mavr: Code reuse stealthy attacks and mitigation on unmanned aerial vehicles. In *IEEE 35th International Conference on Distributed Computing Systems*, pages 642–652, 2015. DOI: 10.1109/icdcs.2015.71. 53

[117] Dina Hadžiosmanović, Robin Sommer, Emmanuele Zambon, and Pieter H. Hartel. Through the eye of the PLC: Semantic security monitoring for industrial processes. In *ACSAC*, 2014. DOI: 10.1145/2664243.2664277. 56, 58, 59

[118] Paul Halliday. The squertproject. http://www.squertproject.org/ 105

[119] D. Halperin, T. S. Heydt-Benjamin, B. Ransford, S. S. Clark, B. Defend, W. Morgan, K. Fu, T. Kohno, and W. H. Maisel. Pacemakers and implantable cardiac defibrillators: Software radio attacks and zero-power defenses. In *IEEE Symposium on Security and Privacy (SP)*, pages 129–142, May 2008. DOI: 10.1109/sp.2008.31. 94

[120] Proof sketch of the halting problem. https://en.wikipedia.org/wiki/Halting_problem%23Sketch_of_proof 4

[121] Andrew Hay, Daniel Cid, and Rory Bray. *OSSEC Host-based Intrusion Detection Guide*. Syngress Publishing, 2008. 105

[122] The heartbleed bug. http://heartbleed.com/ 14, 29

[123] D. Hermanowski. Open source security information management system supporting it security audit. In *IEEE 2nd International Conference on Cybernetics (CYBCONF)*, pages 336–341, June 2015. DOI: 10.1109/cybconf.2015.7175956. 105

[124] HMM-based anomaly detection code and datasets. http://people.cs.vt.edu/danfeng/software.html#HMM-anomaly-detection 96

[125] Grant Ho, Aashish Sharma, Mobin Javed, Vern Paxson, and David Wagner. Detecting credential spearphishing in enterprise settings. In *26th Security Symposium (Security 17)*, pages 469–485, USENIX Association, Vancouver, BC, 2017. 1

[126] Steven A. Hofmeyr, Stephanie Forrest, and Anil Somayaji. Intrusion detection using sequences of system calls. *Journal of Computer Security*, 6(3):151–180, 1998. DOI: 10.3233/jcs-980109. 25

[127] Martin Holste. Elsa. https://github.com/mcholste/elsa 105

[128] Susan Horwitz, Thomas Reps, and David Binkley. Interprocedural slicing using dependence graphs. *ACM Transactions on Programming Languages and Systems*, 12:26–60, 1990. DOI: 10.1145/77606.77608. 45

[129] Hong Hu, Zheng Leong Chua, Sendroiu Adrian, Prateek Saxena, and Zhenkai Liang. Automatic generation of data-oriented exploits. In *24th Security Symposium (Security 15)*, pages 177–192, USENIX Association, Washington, DC, 2015. 28

[130] Hong Hu, Shweta Shinde, Sendroiu Adrian, Zheng Leong Chua, Prateek Saxena, and Zhenkai Liang. Data-oriented programming: On the expressiveness of non-control data attacks. In *Symposium on Security and Privacy, (SP)*, pages 969–986, IEEE Computer Society, San Jose, CA, May 22–26, 2016, DOI: 10.1109/sp.2016.62. 5, 6, 9, 14, 28, 53

[131] L. Huang, A. Joseph, B. Nelson, B. Rubenstein, and J. D. Tygar. Adversarial machine learning. In *Proc. of 4th ACM Workshop on Artificial Intelligence and Security (AISec)*, pages 43–58, October 2011. DOI: 10.1145/2046684.2046692. 97

[132] N. Hubballi, S. Biswas, and S. Nandi. Sequencegram: N-gram modeling of system calls for program based anomaly detection. In *Proc. of the International Conference on Communication Systems and Networks*, pages 1–10, January 2011. DOI: 10.1109/comsnets.2011.5716416. 29

[133] A. Humayed, J. Lin, F. Li, and B. Luo. Cyber-physical systems security—a survey. *IEEE Internet of Things Journal*, PP(99):1–1, 2017. DOI: 10.1109/jiot.2017.2703172. 53

[134] SIGCOMM Internet Traffic Archive (ITA). http://ita.ee.lbl.gov/index.html 97

[135] IBM. IBM cognitive security—Watson for cyber security. https://www.ibm.com/security/cognitive/ 108

[136] The industrial control systems cyber emergency response team. https://ics-cert.us-cert.gov/ 53

[137] Netflix Inc. Surus. https://github.com/Netflix/Surus 106

[138] Netflix Inc. RAD—outlier detection on big data, February 2015. The Netflix Tech Blog. http://techblog.netflix.com/2015/02/rad-outlier-detection-on-big-data.html 1, 6, 106

[139] Splunk Inc. Operational intelligence, log management, application management, enterprise security and compliance | splunk. https://www.splunk.com/ 6, 106

[140] Tripwire Inc. Open source Tripwire. https://github.com/Tripwire/tripwire-open-source 105

[141] Visa Inc. Visa advances cardholder security through improved fraud detection, January 2011. https://usa.visa.com/about-visa/newsroom/press-releases.releaseId.1513794.html 99

[142] Intel 64 and IA-32 architectures software developer's manual. Volume 3C: System programming guide, Part 3. Chapter 36. 9

[143] Identity theft resource center. http://www.idtheftcenter.org/ 16

[144] Jafar Haadi Jafarian, Ehab Al-Shaer, and Qi Duan. OpenFlow random host mutation: Transparent moving target defense using software defined networking. In *Proc. of the 1st Workshop on Hot Topics in Software Defined Networks (HotSDN)*, pages 127–132, 2012. DOI: 10.1145/2342441.2342467. 5

[145] Samuel Jero, Hyojeong Lee, and Cristina Nita-Rotaru. Leveraging state information for automated attack discovery in transport protocol implementations. In *45th Annual IEEE/IFIP International Conference on Dependable Systems and Networks, (DSN)*, pages 1–12, Rio de Janeiro, Brazil, June 22–25, IEEE Computer Society, 2015. DOI: 10.1109/dsn.2015.22. 15

[146] Yunhan Jack Jia, Qi Alfred Chen, Shiqi Wang, Amir Rahmati, Earlence Fernandes, Z. Morley Mao, and Atul Prakash. ContexIoT: Towards providing contextual integrity to appified IoT platforms. In *Network and Distributed System Security Symposium (NDSS)*, 2017. DOI: 10.14722/ndss.2017.23051. 58

[147] Melvin Johnson, Mike Schuster, Quoc V. Le, Maxim Krikun, Yonghui Wu, Zhifeng Chen, Nikhil Thorat, Fernanda B. Viégas, Martin Wattenberg, Greg Corrado, Macduff Hughes, and Jeffrey Dean. Google's multilingual neural machine translation system: Enabling zero-shot translation. *CoRR*, abs/1611.04558, 2016. 10

[148] A. Jones and Y. Lin. Application intrusion detection using language library calls. In *Proc. of the 17th Annual Computer Security Applications Conference, (ACSAC'01)*, IEEE Computer Society, Washington, DC, 2001. DOI: 10.1109/acsac.2001.991561. 25

[149] Sandeep Karanth, Srivatsan Laxman, Prasad Naldurg, Ramarathnam Venkatesan, J. Lambert, and Jinwook Shin. Pattern mining for future attacks. Technical Report MSR-TR-2010-100, Microsoft Research, 2010. 29

[150] Alexander Kedrowitsch. Deceptive environments for cybersecurity defense on low-power devices. Master's thesis, Virginia Tech, Blacksburg, VA, 2017. 5

[151] Arun Kejariwal. Introducing practical and robust anomaly detection in a time series, January 2015. Twitter. https://blog.twitter.com/2015/introducing-practical-and-robust-anomaly-detection-in-a-time-series 1, 6, 106, 112

[152] Wael Khreich, Eric Granger, Ali Miri, and Robert Sabourin. A survey of techniques for incremental learning of HMM parameters. *Information Science*, 197:105–130, August 2012. DOI: 10.1016/j.ins.2012.02.017. 10, 81

[153] Dongsun Kim, Jaechang Nam, Jaewoo Song, and Sunghun Kim. Automatic patch generation learned from human-written patches. In *Proc. of the International Conference on Software Engineering (ICSE)*, 2013. DOI: 10.1109/icse.2013.6606626. 111

[154] Gyuwan Kim, Hayoon Yi, Jangho Lee, Yunheung Paek, and Sungroh Yoon. LSTM-based system-call language modeling and robust ensemble method for designing host-based intrusion detection systems, 2016. Preprint. https://arxiv.org/pdf/1611.01726.pdf 110

[155] Samuel T. King, Zhuoqing Morley Mao, Dominic G. Lucchetti, and Peter M. Chen. Enriching intrusion alerts through multi-host causality. In *Annual Network and Distributed System Security Symposium, (NDSS)*, 2005. 67, 68, 70

[156] Andi Kleen and Beeman Strong. Intel processor trace on linux, 2015. http://tracingsummit.org/w/images/b/b7/TracingSummit2015-IntelPTLinux.pdf 93

[157] J. Z. Kolter and M. A. Maloof. Learning to detect and classify malicious executables in the wild. *Journal of Machine Learning Research*, 7:2721–2744, 2006. 25

[158] David Kushner. The real story of stuxnet. *IEEE Spectrum*, 50(3):48–53, 2013. DOI: 10.1109/mspec.2013.6471059. 53

[159] LBNL/ICSI enterprise network traffic dataset. http://www.icir.org/enterprise-tracing/Overview.html 97

[160] J. Lakonishok and I. Lee. Are insider trades informative? *The Review of Financial Studies*, 14(1):79–111, 2001. DOI: 10.1093/rfs/14.1.79. 1, 2

[161] Jeffrey P. Lanza. SSH CRC32 attack detection code contains remote integer overflow, 2001. Vulnerability notes database. https://www.kb.cert.org/vuls/id/945216 14

[162] Nikolay Laptev, Saeed Amizadeh, and Ian Flint. Generic and scalable framework for automated time-series anomaly detection. In *Proc. of the 21th ACM SIGKDD International Conference on Knowledge Discovery and Data Mining*, pages 1939–1947, 2015. DOI: 10.1145/2783258.2788611. 106

[163] Per Larsen, Stefan Brunthaler, Lucas Davi, Ahmad-Reza Sadeghi, and Michael Franz. *Automated Software Diversity*. Synthesis Lectures on Information Security, Privacy, and Trust. Morgan & Claypool Publishers, 2015. DOI: 10.2200/s00686ed1v01y201512spt014. 5

[164] Pavel Laskov and Nedim Srndic. Static detection of malicious JavaScript-bearing PDF documents. In Robert H'obbes' Zakon, John P. McDermott, and Michael E. Locasto, Eds., *27th Annual Computer Security Applications Conference, (ACSAC)*, pages 373–382, ACM, Orlando, FL, December 5–9, 2011. 25

[165] Wenke Lee and Salvatore J. Stolfo. Data mining approaches for intrusion detection. In *Proc. of the USENIX Security Symposium*, 1998. DOI: 10.21236/ada401496. 8, 29

[166] Wenke Lee, S. J. Stolfo, and K. W. Mok. A data mining framework for building intrusion detection models. In *Security and Privacy, Proc. of the IEEE Symposium on*, pages 120–132, 1999. DOI: 10.1109/secpri.1999.766909. 8

[167] N. G. Leveson and C. S. Turner. An investigation of the Therac-25 accidents. *Computer*, 26(7):18–41, July 1993. DOI: 10.1109/mc.1993.274940. 13

[168] John Leyden. U.S. killer spy drone controls switch to Linux: Flying assassins upgraded after Windows virus outbreak, 2012. http://www.theregister.co.uk/2012/01/12/drone_consoles_linux_switch/ 5

[169] Peng Li, Debin Gao, and Michael K. Reiter. Automatically adapting a trained anomaly detector to software patches. In Engin Kirda, Somesh Jha, and Davide Balzarotti, Eds., *Proc. of the Recent Advances in Intrusion Detection, 12th International Symposium, (RAID)*, Saint-Malo, France, September 23–25, volume 5758 of *Lecture Notes in Computer Science*, pages 142–160, Springer, 2009. DOI: 10.1007/978-3-642-04342-0. 80

[170] Xiaolei Li, Jiawei Han, and Sangkyum Kim. *Motion-Alert: Automatic Anomaly Detection in Massive Moving Objects*, pages 166–177. Springer Berlin Heidelberg, Berlin, Heidelberg, 2006. DOI: 10.1007/11760146_15. 1

[171] Richard Lippmann, Joshua W. Haines, David J. Fried, Jonathan Korba, and Kumar Das. Analysis and results of the 1999 DARPA off-line intrusion detection evaluation. In Hervé Debar, Ludovic Mé, and Shyhtsun Felix Wu, Eds., *Proc. of the Recent Advances in Intrusion Detection, 3rd International Workshop, (RAID)*, Toulouse, France, October 2–4, volume 1907 of *Lecture Notes in Computer Science*, pages 162–182, Springer, 2000. DOI: 10.1007/3-540-39945-3. 97

[172] Fang Liu, Haipeng Cai, Gang Wang, Danfeng Yao, Karim O. Elish, and Barbara G. Ryder. A scalable and prioritized analysis of inter-app communication risks. In *Proc. of the Mobile Security Technologies (MoST) Workshop, in Conjunction with the IEEE Symposium on Security and Privacy*, San Jose, CA, 2017. 45

[173] Fang Liu, Xiaokui Shu, Danfeng Yao, and Ali Raza Butt. Privacy-preserving scanning of big content for sensitive data exposure with MapReduce. In *Proc. of the 5th ACM Conference on Data and Application Security and Privacy, (CODASPY)*, pages 195–206, San Antonio, TX, March 2–4, 2015. DOI: 10.1145/2699026.2699106. 17, 25, 71, 84

[174] Xue Liu, Qixin Wang, Sathish Gopalakrishnan, Wenbo He, Lui Sha, Hui Ding, and Kihwal Lee. ORTEGA: An efficient and flexible online fault tolerance architecture for real-time control systems. *IEEE Transactions on Industrial Informatics*, 4(4):213–224, 2008. DOI: 10.1109/ecrts.2008.17. 14

[175] Yao Liu, Peng Ning, and Michael K. Reiter. False data injection attacks against state estimation in electric power grids. In *CCS*, 2009. DOI: 10.1145/1653662.1653666. 57, 59

[176] M. E. Locasto, J. J. Parekh, A. D. Keromytis, and S. J. Stolfo. Towards collaborative security and P2P intrusion detection. In *Proc. from the 6th Annual IEEE SMC Information Assurance Workshop*, pages 333–339, June 2005. DOI: 10.1109/iaw.2005.1495971. 71

[177] Fan Long and Martin Rinard. Automatic patch generation by learning correct code. In *Proc. of the 43rd Annual ACM SIGPLAN-SIGACT Symposium on Principles of Programming Languages (POPL)*, St. Petersburg, FL, 2016. DOI: 10.1145/2837614.2837617. 111

[178] J. H. Lorie and V. Niederhoffer. Predictive and statistical properties of insider trading. *Journal of Law and Economics*, 11(1):35–53, 1968. DOI: 10.1086/466642. 1, 2, 16

[179] Sixing Lu and Roman Lysecky. Analysis of control flow events for timing-based runtime anomaly detection. In *Proc. of Workshop on Embedded Systems Security*, 2015. DOI: 10.1145/2818362.2818365. 53, 55

[180] M57 Patents enterprise network traffic dataset. `http://digitalcorpora.org/corpora/scenarios/m57-patents-scenario` 97

[181] Shiqing Ma, Juan Zhai, Fei Wang, Kyu Hyung Lee, Xiangyu Zhang, and Dongyan Xu. MPI: Multiple perspective attack investigation with semantic aware execution partitioning. In *26th Security Symposium (Security 17)*, pages 1111–1128, USENIX Association, Vancouver, BC, 2017. 113

[182] Emaad A. Manzoor, Sadegh M. Milajerdi, and Leman Akoglu. Fast memory-efficient anomaly detection in streaming heterogeneous graphs. In Balaji Krishnapuram, Mohak Shah, Alexander J. Smola, Charu Aggarwal, Dou Shen, and Rajeev Rastogi, Eds., *Proc. of the 22nd ACM SIGKDD International Conference on Knowledge Discovery and Data Mining*, pages 1035–1044, San Francisco, CA, August 13–17, 2016. 1

[183] Enrico Mariconti, Lucky Onwuzurike, Panagiotis Andriotis, Emiliano De Cristofaro, Gordon J. Ross, and Gianluca Stringhini. MaMaDroid: Detecting Android malware by building Markov chains of behavioral models. In *Proc. of the Network and Distributed System Security (NDSS) Symposium*, 2017. DOI: 10.14722/ndss.2017.23353. 91

[184] DOD mobility application store (MAS). `http://www.disa.mil/Enterprise-Services/Mobility/DOD-Mobility/Apps` 45

[185] Data exfiltration study: Actors, tactics, and detection. `https://www.mcafee.com/us/resources/reports/rp-data-exfiltration.pdf` 16, 17

[186] John McHugh. Testing intrusion detection systems: A critique of the 1998 and 1999 DARPA intrusion detection system evaluations as performed by Lincoln laboratory. *ACM Transactions on Information and System Security*, 3(4):262–294, November 2000. DOI: 10.1145/382912.382923. 97

[187] Stephen McLaughlin. CPS: Stateful policy enforcement for control system device usage. In *Proc. of the 29th Annual Computer Security Applications Conference, (ACSAC'13)*, pages 109–118, 2013. DOI: 10.1145/2523649.2523673. 56

[188] Stephen McLaughlin, Devin Pohly, Patrick McDaniel, and Saman Zonouz. A trusted safety verifier for process controller code. In *NDSS*, 2014. DOI: 10.14722/ndss.2014.23043. 54, 55, 63

[189] Tony Mecia. Poll: Credit card fraud alerts surge, false alarms still common, 2017. 99

[190] Shagufta Mehnaz and Elisa Bertino. Ghostbuster: A fine-grained approach for anomaly detection in file system accesses. In *ACM Conference on Data and Application Security and Privacy (CODASPY)*, Scottsdale, AZ, 2017. DOI: 10.1145/3029806.3029809. 1

[191] Protecting customers and evaluating risk, April 2017. Microsoft security response center (MSRC). https://blogs.technet.microsoft.com/msrc/2017/04/14/prot ecting-customers-and-evaluating-risk/ 4

[192] R. Mitchell and I.-R. Chen. Behavior rule specification-based intrusion detection for safety critical medical cyber physical systems. *IEEE Transactions on Dependable and Secure Computing*, 12(1):16–30, 2015. DOI: 10.1109/tdsc.2014.2312327. 54

[193] Robert Mitchell and Ing-Ray Chen. Adaptive intrusion detection of malicious unmanned air vehicles using behavior rule specifications. *IEEE Transactions on Systems, Man, and Cybernetics: Systems*, 44(5):593–604, 2014. DOI: 10.1109/tsmc.2013.2265083. 54

[194] Sibin Mohan, Stanley Bak, Emiliano Betti, Heechul Yun, Lui Sha, and Marco Caccamo. S3A: Secure system simplex architecture for enhanced security and robustness of cyber-physical systems. In *HiCoNS*, 2013. DOI: 10.1145/2461446.2461456. 55

[195] NETRESEC publicly available PCAP files. 96

[196] N-gram and FSA anomaly detection labs. http://people.cs.vt.edu/danfeng/sof tware.html#anomaly-detection-lab 96

[197] A. Natarajan, P. Ning, Y. Liu, S. Jajodia, and S. E. Hutchinson. NSDMiner: Automated discovery of network service dependencies. In *Proc. of INFOCOM*, pages 2507–2515, IEEE, 2012. DOI: 10.1109/infcom.2012.6195642. 69

[198] Navy civilian engineer sentenced to 11 years for attempted espionage, 2015. U.S. Department of Justice. https://www.fbi.gov/contact-us/field-offices/norfolk/news/press-releases/navy-civilian-engineer-sentenced-to-11-years-for-attempted-espionage 16

[199] National Cybersecurity and Communications Integration Center (NCCIC). Department of Homeland Security (DHS). 100

[200] Zhenyu Ning and Fengwei Zhang. Ningja: Towards transparent tracing and debugging on ARM. In *Proc. of the 26th USENIX Security Symposium*, Vancouver, Canada, August 2017. 59, 93, 94

[201] B. Niu and G. Tan. Modular control flow integrity. In *Proc. of ACM Conference on Programming Language Design and Implementation (PLDI'14)*, 2014. DOI: 10.1145/2594291.2594295. 8

[202] B. Niu and G. Tan. Per-input control-flow integrity. In *Proc. of 22nd ACM Conference on Computer and Communication Security (CCS)*, October 2015. DOI: 10.1145/2810103.2813644. 8

[203] Node.js. https://nodejs.org/en/ 10

[204] Outlier detection datasets (ODDS). http://odds.cs.stonybrook.edu/ 96

[205] Chetan Parampalli, R. Sekar, and Rob Johnson. A practical mimicry attack against powerful system-call monitors. In *Proc. of ACM ASIACCS*, pages 156–167, 2008. DOI: 10.1145/1368310.1368334. 7, 18

[206] J. J. Parekh. *Privacy-preserving Distributed Event Corroboration*. Ph.D. thesis, Columbia University, 2007. 84

[207] Janak Parekh, Ke Wang, and Salvatore J. Stolfo. Privacy-preserving payload-based correlation for accurate malicious traffic detection. In *Proc. of the SIGCOMM Workshop on Large Scale Attack Defense*, 2006. DOI: 10.1145/1162666.1162667. 84

[208] Young Hee Park and Salvatore J. Stolfo. Software decoys for insider threat. In *ASIACCS*, pages 93–94, 2012. DOI: 10.1145/2414456.2414511. 17

[209] P. Parveen and B. Thuraisingham. Unsupervised incremental sequence learning for insider threat detection. In *IEEE International Conference on Intelligence and Security Informatics*, pages 141–143, June 2012. DOI: 10.1109/isi.2012.6284271. 79

[210] Vern Paxson. Bro: A system for detecting network intruders in real-time. In *Proc. of the 7th Conference on Security Symposium (SSYM'98)* volume 7, USENIX Association, Berkeley, CA, 1998. DOI: 10.1016/s1389-1286(99)00112-7. 105

[211] J. Pearl. *Causality: Models, Reasoning, and Inference*. Cambridge University Press, 2000. DOI: 10.1017/cbo9780511803161. 69

[212] F. Pedregosa, G. Varoquaux, A. Gramfort, V. Michel, B. Thirion, O. Grisel, M. Blondel, P. Prettenhofer, R. Weiss, V. Dubourg, J. Vanderplas, A. Passos, D. Cournapeau, M. Brucher, M. Perrot, and E. Duchesnay. Scikit-learn: Machine learning in Python. *Journal of Machine Learning Research*, 12:2825–2830, 2011. 104

[213] Kexin Pei, Zhongshu Gu, Brendan Saltaformaggio, Shiqing Ma, Fei Wang, Zhiwei Zhang, Luo Si, Xiangyu Zhang, and Dongyan Xu. HERCULE: Attack story reconstruction via community discovery on correlated log graph. In Stephen Schwab, William K. Robertson, and Davide Balzarotti, Eds., *Proc. of the 32nd Annual Conference on Computer Security Applications, ACSAC*, pages 583–595, ACM, Los Angeles, CA, December 5–9, 2016. 70

[214] R. Perdisci, Guofei Gu, and Wenke Lee. Using an ensemble of one-class SVM classifiers to harden payload-based anomaly detection systems. In *Proc. of the International Conference on Data Mining*, pages 488–498, December 2006. DOI: 10.1109/icdm.2006.165. 6

[215] Roberto Perdisci. Useful public resources. `http://roberto.perdisci.com/useful-links` 97

[216] Roberto Perdisci, Davide Ariu, Prahlad Fogla, Giorgio Giacinto, and Wenke Lee. McPAD : A multiple classifier system for accurate payload-based anomaly detection. *Computer Networks, Special Issue on Traffic Classification and its Applications to Modern Networks*, 5(6):864–881, 2009. DOI: 10.1016/j.comnet.2008.11.011. 67

[217] Opto 22 connects real-world industrial devices to millions of Raspberry Pi. `www.prweb.com/releases/2016/11/prweb13853953.htm` 66

[218] Martin Pohlack, Björn Döbel, Adam Lackorzyński, and Technische Universität Dresden. Towards runtime monitoring in real-time systems. In *Proc. of the 8th Real-time Linux Workshop*, 2006. 66

[219] Leonid Portnoy, Eleazar Eskin, and Sal Stolfo. Intrusion detection with unlabeled data using clustering. In *Proc. of ACM CSS Workshop on Data Mining Applied to Security (DMSA)*, pages 5–8, 2001. 21

[220] Aravind Prakash, Heng Yin, and Zhenkai Liang. Enforcing system-wide control flow integrity for exploit detection and diagnosis. In *Proc. of the 8th ACM SIGSAC Symposium on Information, Computer and Communications Security, (ASIA CCS'13)*, pages 311–322, New York, 2013. DOI: 10.1145/2484313.2484352. 8

[221] RIPE routing information service BGP dataset. `http://www.ripe.net/projects/ris/rawdata.html` 97

[222] L. R. Rabiner. A tutorial on hidden Markov models and selected applications in speech recognition. *Proc. of the IEEE*, 77(2):257–286, February 1989. DOI: 10.1109/5.18626. 2, 26

[223] Sazzadur Rahaman and Danfeng Yao. Program analysis of cryptography implementations for security. In *Proc. of IEEE Secure Development Conference (SecDev)*, Cambridge, MA, September 2017. 6

[224] Tabish Rashid, Ioannis Agrafiotis, and Jason R. C. Nurse. A new take on detecting insider threats: Exploring the use of hidden Markov models. In *Proc. of the 8th ACM CCS International Workshop on Managing Insider Security Threats, (MIST'16)*, pages 47–56, New York, 2016. DOI: 10.1145/2995959.2995964. 26

[225] Sharon Reed. Visa cyber fusion center opens in Ashburn, 2016. https://patch.com/virginia/ashburn/visa-cyber-fusion-center-opens-ashburn-0 100

[226] The REX control system for Raspberry Pi. www.rexcontrols.com/ 66

[227] Konrad Rieck, Tammo Krueger, and Andreas Dewald. Cujo: Efficient detection and prevention of drive-by-download attacks. In Gates et al. [102], pages 31–39. DOI: 10.1145/1920261.1920267. 25

[228] Ryan Roemer, Erik Buchanan, Hovav Shacham, and Stefan Savage. Return-oriented programming: Systems, languages, and applications. *ACM Transactions on Information and System Security*, 15(1):2:1–2:34, March 2012. DOI: 10.1145/2133375.2133377. 5, 18

[229] Martin Roesch. Snort—Lightweight intrusion detection for networks. In *Proc. of the 13th Conference on System Administration, (LISA'99)*, pages 229–238, USENIX Association, Berkeley, CA, 1999. 102

[230] Ishtiaq Rouf, Rob Miller, Hossen Mustafa, Travis Taylor, Sangho Oh, Wenyuan Xu, Marco Gruteser, Wade Trappe, and Ivan Seskar. Security and privacy vulnerabilities of in-car wireless networks: A tire pressure monitoring system case study. In *USENIX Security*, 2010. 54

[231] Benjamin Sangster, T. J. O'Connor, Thomas Cook, Robert Fanelli, Erik Dean, William J. Adams, Chris Morrell, and Gregory Conti. Toward instrumenting network warfare competitions to generate labeled datasets. In *Proc. of the 2nd Conference on Cyber Security Experimentation and Test, (CSET'09)*, USENIX Association, Berkeley, CA, 2009. 97

[232] M. Schwartz, J. Mulder, A. R. Chavez, and B. A. Allan. Emerging techniques for field device security. *IEEE Security and Privacy*, 12(6):24–31, 2014. DOI: 10.1109/msp.2014.114. 52, 66

[233] IBM security. IBM cyber security intelligence index, July 2015. 100

[234] LLC security onion solutions. Security onion. https://securityonion.net/ 105

[235] R. Sekar, M. Bendre, D. Dhurjati, and P. Bollineni. A fast automaton-based method for detecting anomalous program behaviors. In *Proc. of the Symposium on Security and Privacy, (SP'01)*, IEEE Computer Society, Washington, DC, 2001. DOI: 10.1109/secpri.2001.924295. 8, 27, 37

[236] R. Sekar, Mugdha Bendre, Dinakar Dhurjati, and Pradeep Bollineni. A fast automaton-based method for detecting anomalous program behaviors. In *Proc. of the IEEE Symposium on Security and Privacy*, pages 144–155, 2001. DOI: 10.1109/secpri.2001.924295. 6

[237] Ted E. Senator, Henry G. Goldberg, Alex Memory, William T. Young, Brad Rees, Robert Pierce, Daniel Huang, Matthew Reardon, David A. Bader, Edmond Chow, Irfan Essa, Joshua Jones, Vinay Bettadapura, Duen Horng Chau, Oded Green, Oguz Kaya, Anita Zakrzewska, Erica Briscoe, Rudolph IV L. Mappus, Robert McColl, Lora Weiss, Thomas G. Dietterich, Alan Fern, Weng-Keen Wong, Shubhomoy Das, Andrew Emmott, Jed Irvine, Jay-Yoon Lee, Danai Koutra, Christos Faloutsos, Daniel Corkill, Lisa Friedland, Amanda Gentzel, and David Jensen. Detecting insider threats in a real corporate database of computer usage activity. In *Proc. of the 19th ACM SIGKDD International Conference on Knowledge Discovery and Data Mining, (KDD'13)*, pages 1393–1401, ACM, New York, 2013. DOI: 10.1145/2487575.2488213. 1, 16, 17, 97, 114

[238] Hovav Shacham. The geometry of innocent flesh on the bone: Return-into-libc without function calls (on the x86). In Peng Ning, Sabrina De Capitani di Vimercati, and Paul F. Syverson, Eds., *Proc. of the Conference on Computer and Communications Security, (CCS)*, pages 552–561, ACM, Alexandria, VA, October 28–31, 2007. 5, 8, 18

[239] Hovav Shacham, Matthew Page, Ben Pfaff, Eu-Jin Goh, Nagendra Modadugu, and Dan Boneh. On the effectiveness of address-space randomization. In *Proc. of the ACM Conference on Computer and Communications Security*, pages 298–307, 2004. DOI: 10.1145/1030083.1030124. 14, 29

[240] Noah Shachtman. Exclusive: Computer virus hits U.S. drone fleet, 2011. https://www.wired.com/2011/10/virus-hits-drone-fleet/ 5

[241] The shadow brokers. https://en.wikipedia.org/wiki/The_Shadow_Brokers 4

[242] Abhishek B. Sharma, Franjo Ivančić, Alexandru Niculescu-Mizil, Haifeng Chen, and Guofei Jiang. Modeling and analytics for cyber-physical systems in the age of big data. *SIGMETRICS Performance Evaluation Review*, 41(4):74–77, 2014. DOI: 10.1145/2627534.2627558. 51

[243] Manali Sharma, Kamalika Das, Mustafa Bilgic, Bryan Matthews, David Nielsen, and Nikunj Oza. Active learning with rationales for identifying operationally significant anomalies in aviation. In *Proc. of the Machine Learning and Knowledge Discovery in Databases: European Conference, (ECML PKDD) Part III*, pages 209–225, Springer International Publishing, Riva del Garda, Italy, September 19–23, Cham, 2016. DOI: 10.1007/978-3-319-46131-1_25. 1

[244] Xiaokui Shu. *Threat Detection in Program Execution and Data Movement: Theory and Practice*. Ph.D. thesis, Virginia Tech, 2016. vi

[245] Xiaokui Shu, Nikolay Laptev, and Danfeng Yao. DECT: Distributed evolving context tree for understanding user behavior pattern evolution. In *Proc. of 19th International Conference on Extending Database Technology (EDBT)*, Bordeaux, France, March 2016. 112

[246] Xiaokui Shu and Danfeng Yao. Data leak detection as a service. In *Proc. of the International Conference on Security and Privacy in Communication Networks (SecureComm)*, 2012. DOI: 10.1007/978-3-642-36883-7_14. 17, 25

[247] Xiaokui Shu and Danfeng Yao. Program anomaly detection: Methodology and practices. In Edgar R. Weippl, Stefan Katzenbeisser, Christopher Kruegel, Andrew C. Myers, and Shai Halevi, Eds., *Proc. of the ACM SIGSAC Conference on Computer and Communications Security*, pages 1853–1854, Vienna, Austria, October 24–28, 2016. 96

[248] Xiaokui Shu, Danfeng Yao, and Elisa Bertino. Privacy-preserving detection of sensitive data exposure. *IEEE Transactions on Information Forensics and Security*, 10(5):1092–1103, 2015. DOI: 10.1109/tifs.2015.2398363. 17, 25

[249] Xiaokui Shu, Danfeng Yao, and Naren Ramakrishnan. Unearthing stealthy program attacks buried in extremely long execution paths. In *Proc. of the 22nd ACM SIGSAC Conference on Computer and Communications Security (CCS)*, October 2015. DOI: 10.1145/2810103.2813654. 1, 6, 8, 9, 19, 21, 22, 23, 27, 31, 34, 58, 91, 92

[250] Xiaokui Shu, Danfeng Yao, Naren Ramakrishnan, and Trent Jaeger. Long-span program behavior modeling and attack detection. *ACM Transactions on Privacy and Security (TOPS)*, 2017. 6, 22, 23, 27, 31, 32, 33, 34, 94

[251] Xiaokui Shu, Danfeng Yao, and Barbara Ryder. A formal framework for program anomaly detection. In *Proc. of the 18th International Symposium on Research in Attacks, Intrusions and Defenses (RAID)*, Kyoto, Japan, November 2015. DOI: 10.1007/978-3-319-26362-5_13. 6, 25, 27, 48, 49

[252] Xiaokui Shu, Jing Zhang, Danfeng (Daphne) Yao, and Wu-chun Feng. Fast detection of transformed data leaks. *IEEE Transactions on Information Forensics and Security*, 11(3):528–542, 2016. DOI: 10.1109/tifs.2015.2503271. 17, 25

[253] Software-artifact Infrastructure Repository (SIR). http://sir.unl.edu/portal/index.php 37, 91

[254] Tony C. Smith and Eibe Frank. *Statistical Genomics: Methods and Protocols*, chapter: Introducing Machine Learning Concepts with WEKA, pages 353–378, Springer, New York, 2016. DOI: 10.1007/978-1-4939-3578-9_17. 104

[255] Kevin Z. Snow, Fabian Monrose, Lucas Davi, Alexandra Dmitrienko, Christopher Liebchen, and Ahmad-Reza Sadeghi. Just-in-time code reuse: On the effectiveness of fine-grained address space layout randomization. In *Proc. of the Symposium on Security and Privacy*, IEEE Computer Society, 2013. DOI: 10.1109/sp.2013.45. 5, 18

[256] Solar designer. return-to-libc attack, August 1997. Bugtraq. 18

[257] Anil Somayaji and Stephanie Forrest. Automated response using system-call delays. In *Proc. of the 9th Conference on Security Symposium (SSYM'00)*, volume 9, USENIX Association, Berkeley, CA, 2000. 18

[258] C. Song, B. Lee, K. Lu, W. R. Harris, T. Kim, and W. Lee. Enforcing Kernel security invariants with data flow integrity. In *Proc. of the 23th Annual Network and Distributed System Security Symposium (NDSS)*, 2016. DOI: 10.14722/ndss.2016.23218. 5

[259] Alexander Sotirov. Heap Feng Shui in JavaScript, 2007. Black Hat Europe. https://www.blackhat.com/presentations/bh-usa-07/Sotirov/Whitepaper/bh-usa-07-sotirov-WP.pdf 14, 29

[260] S. Sparks, S. Embleton, R. Cunningham, and C. Zou. Automated vulnerability analysis: Leveraging control flow for evolutionary input crafting. In *23rd Annual Computer Security Applications Conference, (ACSAC)*, pages 477–486, 2007. DOI: 10.1109/acsac.2007.27. 42

[261] S. Sridhar, A. Hahn, and M. Govindarasu. Cyber-physical system security for the electric power grid. *Proc. of the IEEE*, 100(1):210–224, 2012. DOI: 10.1109/jproc.2011.2165269. 51, 54

[262] Angelos Stavrou, Gabriela F. Cretu-Ciocarlie, Michael E. Locasto, and Salvatore J. Stolfo. Keep your friends close: The necessity for updating an anomaly sensor with legitimate environment changes. In *Proc. of the 2nd ACM Workshop on Security and Artificial Intelligence, (AISec'09)*, pages 39–46, New York, 2009. DOI: 10.1145/1654988.1655000. 10, 79, 80, 81

[263] S. J. Stolfo, M. B. Salem, and A. D. Keromytis.   Fog computing: Mitigating insider data theft attacks in the cloud.   In *IEEE Symposium on Security and Privacy Workshops*, pages 125–128, May 2012. DOI: 10.1109/spw.2012.19. 5, 17

[264] Salvatore J. Stolfo. Anomaly detection: Algorithms, sensors and systems, Payl, Anagram, Spectrogram. `http://www.cs.columbia.edu/~sal/bio.html` 6

[265] Salvatore J. Stolfo. The columbia university intrusion detection systems lab. `http://ids.cs.columbia.edu/` 99

[266] Salvatore J. Stolfo, Angelos D. Keromytis, and Vanessa Frias-Martinez. Behavior-profile clustering for false alert reduction in anomaly detection sensors. In *Proc. of the 13th Asia-Pacific Computer Systems Architecture Conference (ACSAC)*, pages 367–376, 2008. DOI: 10.1109/ACSAC.2008.30. 97

[267] M. Strohmeier, M. Schäfer, M. Smith, V. Lenders, and I. Martinovic. Assessing the impact of aviation security on cyber power. In *8th International Conference on Cyber Conflict (CyCon)*, pages 223–241, May 2016. DOI: 10.1109/cycon.2016.7529437. 13

[268] Acar Tamersoy, Elias Khalil, Bo Xie, Stephen L. Lenkey, Bryan R. Routledge, Duen Horng Chau, and Shamkant B. Navathe. Large scale insider trading analysis: Patterns and discoveries. *Social Network Analysis and Mining (SNAM)*, 4(1):1–17, 2014. DOI: 10.1007/s13278-014-0201-9. 1, 2

[269] J. Tan, H. J. Tay, U. Drolia, R. Gandhi, and P. Narasimhan. PCFIRE: Towards provable preventative control-flow integrity enforcement for realistic embedded software. In *International Conference on Embedded Software (EMSOFT)*, pages 1–10, 2016. DOI: 10.1145/2968478.2968492. 59, 62, 66

[270] Kymie Tan, John McHugh, and Kevin Killourhy. Hiding intrusions: From the abnormal to the normal and beyond. In Fabien A. P. Petitcolas, Ed., *Information Hiding: 5th International Workshop, (IH)* Noordwijkerhout, The Netherlands, October 7–9, 2002 Revised Papers, pages 1–17, Springer Berlin Heidelberg, Berlin, Heidelberg, 2003. DOI: 10.1007/3-540-36415-3. 18

[271] Kymie M. C. Tan, Kevin S. Killourhy, and Roy A. Maxion. Undermining an anomaly-based intrusion detection system using common exploits. In *Proc. of the 5th International Conference on Recent Advances in Intrusion Detection, (RAID'02)*, pages 54–73, Springer-Verlag, Berlin, Heidelberg, 2002. DOI: 10.1007/3-540-36084-0_4. 8, 18

[272] Ying Tan, Mehmet C. Vuran, Steve Goddard, Yue Yu, Miao Song, and Shangping Ren. A concept lattice-based event model for cyber-physical systems. In *ICCPS*, 2010. DOI: 10.1145/1795194.1795202. 51

[273] The CERT division. Insider threat tools. `https://www.cert.org/insider-threat/tools/` 97

[274] Suresh Thummalapenta, Tao Xie, Nikolai Tillmann, Jonathan de Halleux, and Zhendong Su. Synthesizing method sequences for high-coverage testing. In Cristina Videira Lopes and Kathleen Fisher, Eds., *Proc. of the 26th Annual ACM SIGPLAN Conference on Object-Oriented Programming, Systems, Languages, and Applications, (OOPSLA)*, pages 189–206, part of SPLASH 2011, Portland, OR, October 22–27, 2011. 37

[275] Ke Tian, Danfeng Yao, Barbara G. Ryder, and Gang Tan. Analysis of code heterogeneity for high-precision classification of repackaged malware. In *Security and Privacy Workshops, (SP)*, pages 262–271, IEEE Computer Society, San Jose, CA, May 22–26, 2016. DOI: 10.1109/spw.2016.33. 45

[276] A. M. Turing. On computable numbers, with an application to the entscheidungsproblem. *Proc. of the London Mathematical Society*, 42(1):230–265, 1936. DOI: 10.1112/plms/s2-42.1.230. 4

[277] J. D. Tygar. Adversarial machine learning. *IEEE Internet Computing*, 15(5):4–6, September 2011. DOI: 10.1109/mic.2011.112. 97

[278] United States Military Academy (USMA) West Point dataset. `http://www.westpoint.edu/crc/SitePages/DataSets.aspx` 97

[279] University of New Mexico intrusion detection dataset. `https://www.cs.unm.edu/~immsec/systemcalls.htm` 97

[280] Johannes Ullrich. A poor man's DNS anomaly detection script, August 2017. `https://isc.sans.edu/diary/A+Poor+Man's+DNS+Anomaly+Detection+Script/13918` 106

[281] Blase Ur, Elyse McManus, Melwyn Pak Yong Ho, and Michael L. Littman. Practical trigger-action programming in the smart home. In *Proc. of the SIGCHI Conference on Human Factors in Computing Systems, (CHI'14)*, 2014. DOI: 10.1145/2556288.2557420. 58

[282] David I. Urbina, Jairo A. Giraldo, Alvaro A. Cardenas, Nils Ole Tippenhauer, Junia Valente, Mustafa Faisal, Justin Ruths, Richard Candell, and Henrik Sandberg. Limiting the impact of stealthy attacks on industrial control systems. In *Proc. of the ACM Conference on Computer and Communications Security (CCS)*, 2016. DOI: 10.1145/2976749.2978388. 54, 56, 59

[283] Junia Valente, Carlos Barreto, and Alvaro A. Cárdenas. Cyber-physical systems attestation. In *DCOSS*, 2014. DOI: 10.1109/dcoss.2014.61. 65

[284] Adrien Vergé, Naser Ezzati-Jivan, and Michel R. Dagenais. Hardware-assisted software event tracing. *Concurrency and Computation: Practice and Experience*, 29(10):e4069–n/a, 2017. e4069 cpe.4069. DOI: 10.1002/cpe.4069. 66

[285] Data breach investigations report. `http://www.verizonenterprise.com/verizon-insights-lab/dbir/` 16

[286] Giovanni Vigna. Network intrusion detection: Dead or alive? In Gates et al. [102], pages 117–126. DOI: 10.1145/1920261.1920279. 67

[287] Bamm Visscher. Sguil: The analyst console for network security monitoring. `http://bammv.github.io/sguil/` 105

[288] Nedim Šrndić and Pavel Laskov. Practical evasion of a learning-based classifier: A case study. In *Proc. of the Symposium on Security and Privacy, (SP'14)*, pages 197–211, IEEE Computer Society, Washington, DC, 2014. DOI: 10.1109/SP.2014.20. 113

[289] David Wagner and Drew Dean. Intrusion detection via static analysis. In *Proc. of the Symposium on Security and Privacy, (SP'01)*, IEEE Computer Society, Washington, DC, 2001. DOI: 10.1109/secpri.2001.924296. 6, 8, 38

[290] David Wagner and Paolo Soto. Mimicry attacks on host-based intrusion detection systems. In *Proc. of ACM CCS*, pages 255–264, 2002. DOI: 10.1145/586143.586145. 7, 8, 18, 19

[291] Ke Wang, Janak J. Parekh, and Salvatore J. Stolfo. Anagram: A content anomaly detector resistant to mimicry attack. In Diego Zamboni and Christopher Kruegel, Eds., *Proc. of the Recent Advances in Intrusion Detection: 9th International Symposium, (RAID)*, pages 226–248, Springer Berlin Heidelberg, Hamburg, Germany, September 20–22, Berlin, Heidelberg, 2006. DOI: 10.1007/11856214. 25, 80, 82, 83, 86

[292] Ke Wang and Salvatore J. Stolfo. Anomalous payload-based network intrusion detection. In Erland Jonsson, Alfonso Valdes, and Magnus Almgren, Eds., *Proc. of the Recent Advances in Intrusion Detection: 7th International Symposium, (RAID)*, pages 203–222, Springer Berlin Heidelberg, Sophia Antipolis, France, September 15–17, Berlin, Heidelberg, 2004. DOI: 10.1007/b100714. 19, 21, 22, 67, 80, 82, 97

[293] Yong Wang, Zhaoyan Xu, Jialong Zhang, Lei Xu, Haopei Wang, and Guofei Gu. Srid: State relation based intrusion detection for false data injection attacks in scada. In *ESORICS*, 2014. DOI: 10.1007/978-3-319-11212-1_23. 51, 56

[294] Christina Warrender, Stephanie Forrest, and Barak Pearlmutter. Detecting intrusions using system calls: Alternative data models. In *Proc. of the IEEE Symposium on Security and Privacy*, pages 133–145, 1999. DOI: 10.1109/secpri.1999.766910. 6, 8, 25, 26, 29, 37, 42, 59, 62

[295] IBM Watson IoT Platform. www.ibm.com/internet-of-things/ 60

[296] Britton Wolfe, Karim O. Elish, and Danfeng Yao. High precision screening for android malware with dimensionality reduction. In *13th International Conference on Machine Learning and Applications, (ICMLA)*, pages 21–28, IEEE, Detroit, MI, December 3–6, 2014. DOI: 10.1109/icmla.2014.10. 25, 44

[297] Britton Wolfe, Karim O. Elish, and Danfeng (Daphne) Yao. Comprehensive behavior profiling for proactive android malware detection. In Sherman S. M. Chow, Jan Camenisch, Lucas Chi Kwong Hui, and Siu-Ming Yiu, Eds., *Proc. of the Information Security—17th International Conference, (ISC)*, Hong Kong, China, October 12–14, volume 8783 of *Lecture Notes in Computer Science*, pages 328–344, Springer, 2014. DOI: 10.1007/978-3-319-13257-0. 44

[298] Christian Wressnegger. Salad—an open-source implementation of a content anomaly detector based on N-grams. http://mlsec.org/salad/ 25, 96

[299] Christian Wressnegger, Guido Schwenk, Daniel Arp, and Konrad Rieck. A close look on N-grams in intrusion detection: Anomaly detection vs. classification. In *Proc. of the ACM Workshop on Artificial Intelligence and Security, (AISec'13)*, pages 67–76, New York, 2013. DOI: 10.1145/2517312.2517316. 8, 24, 67

[300] Kui Xu. *Anomaly Detection Through System and Program Behavior Modeling*. PhD thesis, Virginia Tech, 2014. vi

[301] Kui Xu, Patrick Butler, Sudip Saha, and Danfeng Yao. DNS for massive-scale command and control. *IEEE Transactions of Dependable and Secure Computing (TDSC)*, 10(3):143–153, May/June 2013. DOI: 10.1109/tdsc.2013.10. 22, 68

[302] Kui Xu, Ke Tian, Danfeng Yao, and Barbara Ryder. A sharper sense of self: Probabilistic reasoning of program behaviors for anomaly detection with context sensitivity. In *Proc. of the 46th Annual IEEE/IFIP International Conference on Dependable Systems and Networks (DSN)*, June 2016. DOI: 10.1109/dsn.2016.49. 1, 6, 9, 24, 38, 39, 43, 44, 49, 91, 94, 95, 109

[303] Kui Xu, Danfeng Yao, Qiang Ma, and Alexander Crowell. Detecting infection onset with behavior-based policies. In *Proc. of the 5th International Conference on Network and System Security (NSS)*, September 2011. DOI: 10.1109/icnss.2011.6059960. 69, 78

[304] Kui Xu, Danfeng Yao, Barbara Ryder, and Ke Tian. Probabilistic program modeling for high-precision anomaly classification. In *Proc. of the IEEE Computer Security Foundations Symposium (CSF)*, Verona, Italy, July 2015. DOI: 10.1109/csf.2015.37. 1, 6, 8, 9, 24, 38, 39, 40, 41, 42, 49, 59, 62, 81, 91, 94, 109

[305] Weilin Xu, Yanjun Qi, and David Evans. Automatically evading classifiers: A case study on PDF malware classifiers. In *23nd Annual Network and Distributed System Security Symposium, (NDSS)*, The Internet Society, San Diego, CA, February 21–24, 2016. DOI: 10.14722/ndss.2016.23115. 113

[306] Junfeng Yang, Ang Cui, Sal Stolfo, and Simha Sethumadhavan. Raw data of concurrency attacks. `http://systems.cs.columbia.edu/archive/pub/2012/06/concurrency-attacks` 112

[307] Junfeng Yang, Ang Cui, Sal Stolfo, and Simha Sethumadhavan. Concurrency attacks. In *Proc. of the 4th USENIX Workshop on Hot Topics in Parallelism*, Berkeley, CA, 2012. 10, 18, 111, 112

[308] Danfeng Yao. Cloud data analytics for security: Applications, challenges, and opportunities. In *Proc. of Security in Cloud Computing (SCC) Workshop, in conjunction with ASIACCS*, Abu Dhabi, UAE, April 2017. `https://conference.cs.cityu.edu.hk/asi accsscc/17/Yao-SCC-Keynote-2017.pdf` DOI: 10.1145/3055259.3055266. 7, 10

[309] Jianguo Yao, Xue Liu, Guchuan Zhu, and Lui Sha. Netsimplex: Controller fault tolerance architecture in networked control systems. *IEEE Transactions on Industrial Informatics*, 9(1):346–356, 2013. DOI: 10.1109/tii.2012.2219060. 14

[310] Dit-Yan Yeung and Yuxin Ding. Host-based intrusion detection using dynamic and static behavioral models. *Pattern Recognition*, 36(1):229–243, 2003. DOI: 10.1016/s0031-3203(02)00026-2. 26, 42

[311] Heng Yin, Dawn Song, Manuel Egele, Christopher Kruegel, and Engin Kirda. Panorama: Capturing system-wide information flow for malware detection and analysis. In *Proc. of the 14th ACM Conferences on Computer and Communication Security (CCS)*, 2007. DOI: 10.1145/1315245.1315261. 114

[312] Man-Ki Yoon, S. Mohan, Jaesik Choi, Jung-Eun Kim, and Lui Sha. SecureCore: A multicore-based intrusion detection architecture for real-time embedded systems. In *RTAS*, 2013. DOI: 10.1109/rtas.2013.6531076. 55

[313] Man-Ki Yoon, Sibin Mohan, Jaesik Choi, Mihai Christodorescu, and Lui Sha. Learning execution contexts from system call distribution for anomaly detection in smart embedded system. In *Proc. of the 2nd International Conference on Internet-of-things Design and Implementation, (IoTDI'17)*, pages 191–196, 2017. DOI: 10.1145/3054977.3054999. 55, 57, 58

[314] A. Zand, G. Vigna, R. Kemmerer, and C. Kruegel. Rippler: Delay injection for service dependency detection. In *IEEE INFOCOM—Conference on Computer Communications*, pages 2157–2165, April 2014. DOI: 10.1109/infocom.2014.6848158. 67, 69

[315] Kexiong Curtis Zeng, Yuanchao Shu, Shinan Liu, Yanzhi Dou, and Yaling Yang. A practical GPS location spoofing attack in road navigation scenario. In *Proc. of the 18th International Workshop on Mobile Computing Systems and Applications, (HotMobile'17)*, pages 85–90, ACM, New York, 2017. DOI: 10.1145/3032970.3032983. 45

[316] Chao Zhang, Tao Wei, Zhaofeng Chen, Lei Duan, Laszlo Szekeres, Stephen McCamant, Dawn Song, and Wei Zou. Practical control flow integrity and randomization for binary executables. In *IEEE Symposium on Security and Privacy*, pages 559–573, 2013. DOI: 10.1109/sp.2013.44. 8

[317] Hao Zhang. *Discovery of Triggering Relations and Its Applications in Network Security and Android Malware Detection*. Ph.D. thesis, Virginia Tech, 2015. vi

[318] Hao Zhang, Maoyuan Sun, Danfeng (Daphne) Yao, and Chris North. Visualizing traffic causality for analyzing network anomalies. In Stephen Huang and Rakesh M. Verma, Eds., *Proc. of the ACM International Workshop on International Workshop on Security and Privacy Analytics, (IWSPA@CODASPY)*, pages 37–42, San Antonio, TX, March 4, 2015. 76

[319] Hao Zhang, Danfeng Yao, and Naren Ramakrishnan. Detection of stealthy malware activities with traffic causality and scalable triggering relation discovery. In *Proc. of the 9th ACM Symposium on Information, Computer and Communications Security, (ASIACCS)*, pages 39–50, Kyoto, Japan, June 2014. DOI: 10.1145/2590296.2590309. 67, 68, 69, 71, 73, 74, 75

[320] Hao Zhang, Danfeng Yao, Naren Ramakrishnan, and Zhibin Zhang. Causality reasoning about network events for detecting stealthy malware activities. *Computers and Security (CS)*, 58:180–198, 2016. DOI: 10.1016/j.cose.2016.01.002. 67, 69, 71, 73, 74, 76, 77

[321] Hao Zhang, Danfeng (Daphne) Yao, and Naren Ramakrishnan. Causality-based sense-making of network traffic for Android application security. In *Proc. of the ACM Workshop on Artificial Intelligence and Security, (AISec'16)*, pages 47–58, New York, 2016. DOI: 10.1145/2996758.2996760. 44, 67, 69, 78

[322] Mingwei Zhang and R. Sekar. Control flow integrity for COTS binaries. In *Proc. of the 22nd Conference on Security, (SEC'13)*, pages 337–352, USENIX Association, Berkeley, CA, 2013. 8

[323] Xiangyu Zhang, Rajiv Gupta, and Youtao Zhang. Precise dynamic slicing algorithms. In *ICSE'03*, 2003. DOI: 10.1109/icse.2003.1201211. 61

[324] Y. Zhou and X. Jiang. Dissecting Android malware: Characterization and evolution. In *IEEE Symposium on Security and Privacy*, pages 95–109, May 2012. DOI: 10.1109/sp.2012.16. 14

[325] Rui Zhuang, Scott A. DeLoach, and Xinming Ou. Towards a theory of moving target defense. In *Proc. of the 1st ACM Workshop on Moving Target Defense, (MTD'14)*, pages 31–40, New York, 2014. DOI: 10.1145/2663474.2663479. 5

[326] Yanyan Zhuang, Eleni Gessiou, Steven Portzer, Fraida Fund, Monzur Muhammad, Ivan Beschastnikh, and Justin Cappos. Netcheck: Network diagnoses from blackbox traces. In *Proc. of the 11th USENIX Conference on Networked Systems Design and Implementation, (NSDI'14)*, pages 115–128, 2014. 91

[327] Christopher Zimmer, Balasubramanya Bhat, Frank Mueller, and Sibin Mohan. Time-based intrusion detection in cyber-physical systems. In *ICCPS*, 2010. DOI: 10.1145/1795194.1795210. 53, 55, 59

[328] ZingBox: Enabling the Internet of Trusted Things. www.zingbox.com/ 65

Authors' Biographies

DANFENG (DAPHNE) YAO

Danfeng (Daphne) Yao is an Associate Professor of Computer Science at Virginia Tech. In the past decade, she has worked on designing and developing data-driven anomaly detection techniques for securing networked systems against stealthy exploits and attacks. Her expertise also includes software security, mobile security, cloud security, and applied cryptography. Professor Yao received her Ph.D. in Computer Science from Brown University.

Professor Yao is an Elizabeth and James E. Turner Jr. '56 Faculty Fellow and L-3 Faculty Fellow. She received the NSF CAREER Award in 2010 for her work on human-behavior driven malware detection, and the ARO Young Investigator Award for her semantic reasoning for mission-oriented security work in 2014. She received several Best Paper Awards and Best Poster Awards. She was given the Award for Technological Innovation from Brown University in 2006. She holds multiple U.S. patents for her anomaly detection technologies.

Professor Yao is an Associate Editor of *IEEE Transactions on Dependable and Secure Computing (TDSC)*. She serves as the PC member in numerous computer security conferences, including *ACM CCS, IEEE Security & Privacy Symposium*. She has over 85 peer-reviewed publications in major security and privacy conferences and journals. Daphne is an active member of the security research community. She serves as the Secretary/Treasurer at ACM Special Interest Group on Security, Audit and Control (SIGSAC).

XIAOKUI SHU

Xiaokui Shu is a Research Staff Member in the Cognitive Cybersecurity Intelligence Group at the IBM T. J. Watson Research Center. He received his Ph.D. degree in Computer Science from Virginia Tech and a B.S. degree from University of Science and Technology of China (USTC). His research interests are in system and network security, such as intrusion detection, cyber defense, and threat intelligence. He received the Outstanding Ph.D. Student Award from Virginia Tech and the prestigious Guo Moruo Award from USTC. Dr. Shu's research was published in top conferences and journals, including *ACM Conference on Computer and Communications Security (CCS)* and *ACM Transactions on Privacy and Security (TOPS)*. Dr. Shu enjoys cyber security Capture The Flag (CTF) competitions. He won the first prize in the Inaugural Virginia Tech Cyber Security Summit Competition.

LONG CHENG

Long Cheng is currently pursuing his second Ph.D. in the Department of Computer Science at Virginia Tech. His research interests include system and network security, cyber forensics, cyber-physical systems (CPS) security, mobile computing, and wireless networks. He received his first Ph.D. degree from Beijing University of Posts and Telecommunications in 2012. Dr. Cheng received the Best Paper Award from *IEEE Wireless Communications and Networking Conference (WCNC)* in 2013 and the prestigious Erasmus Mundus Scholar Award from the European Union in 2014.

Dr. Cheng's research activities span across the fields of cyber security and networking. He has published over 60 papers in peer-reviewed journals and conferences, including *IEEE Transactions on Information Forensics and Security (TIFS)*, *IEEE/ACM Transactions on Networking (ToN)*, *Annual Computer Security Applications Conference (ACSAC)*, and *Privacy Enhancing Technologies Symposium (PETS)*. He was invited to write a review article on enterprise data breach in Wiley's *WIREs Data Mining and Knowledge Discovery*. Dr. Cheng has extensive experiences collaborating with researchers in the industry and academia across multiple continents. He holds a patent for his sensor network routing method.

SALVATORE J. STOLFO

Salvatore J. Stolfo is a Professor of Computer Science at Columbia University. He received his Ph.D. from NYU Courant Institute in 1979 and has been on the faculty of Columbia ever since. He won the IBM Faculty Development Award early in his academic career in 1983. He has published several books and over 250 scientific papers and received several Best Paper Awards. His research spans across the areas of parallel computing, AI knowledge-based systems, data mining, and most recently computer security and intrusion detection systems.

Professor Stolfo has been granted 33 patents in the areas of parallel computing and database inference and computer security, most of which have been licensed. His research has been supported by DARPA, NSF, ONR, NSA, CIA, IARPA, AFOSR, ARO, NIST, DHS, and numerous companies and state agencies. Professor Stolfo has mentored over 30 Ph.D. students and many Master's students. His most recent research is devoted to payload anomaly detection for zero-day exploits, secure private querying, private and anonymous network trace synthesis, and automatic bait generation for trap-based defense to mitigate the insider threat.

Index

Printed in the United States
by Baker & Taylor Publisher Services